Ulysses as a Comic Novel

D0209645

Irish Studies

Richard Fallis, Series Editor

❧ ULYSSES *as a Comic Novel* ❧

ZACK BOWEN

PROPERTY OF
BAKER COLLEGE OF FLINT

SYRACUSE UNIVERSITY PRESS

Copyright © 1989 by Syracuse University Press
Syracuse, New York 13244-5160

ALL RIGHTS RESERVED

First Edition 1989
99 98 97 96 95 94 93 92 91 90 89   6 5 4 3 2 1

The paper used in this publication meets the minimum requirements of American National Standard for Information Sciences — Permanence of Paper for Printed Library Materials, ANSI Z39.48-1984. ∞™

Library of Congress Cataloging-in-Publication Data

Bowen, Zack R.
    Ulysses as a comic novel / Zack Bowen.— 1st ed.
      p.   cm.—(Irish studies)
    Bibliography: p.
    Includes index.
    ISBN 0-8156-2471-9 (alk. paper)
    1. Joyce, James, 1882–1941. Ulysses. 2. Joyce, James, 1882–1941—
Humor. 3. Comic, The, in literature. I. Title. II. Series:
Irish studies (Syracuse, N.Y.)
PR6019.O9U629 1989   89-32238
823'.912—dc20   CIP

MANUFACTURED IN THE UNITED STATES OF AMERICA

"Of all living creatures only man is endowed with laughter."
—Aristotle, *De Anima,* Book 3, chapter 10

Zack Bowen, Chairman, Department of English, University of Miami, is a distinguished Joycean scholar whose published works include *Padraic Colum* (1970), *Musical Allusions in the Works of James Joyce: Early Poetry Through "Ulysses"* (1974), *Mary Lavin* (1975), and *A Companion to Joyce Studies* (1984). In the 1960s he was Producer-Director of a series of recorded interpretations of *Ulysses*, and he has served in various literary editorships of publications such as *The Irish Renaissance Annual*.

Contents

Texts Used and Abbreviations

P   *A Portrait of the Artist as a Young Man.* New York: Viking, 1971.

U   *"Ulysses": The Corrected Text.* Edited by Hans Walter Gabler with Wolfhard Steppe and Claus Melchior. New York: Random House, 1986.

References to *Ulysses* will signify episodes by number and line. For example, 11:70 – 72 means lines 70 – 72 of the Sirens episode.

For readers' convenience the Gabler citations will be followed by a citation for the parallel passage in the 1961 Random House edition. These page numbers will be designated *1961*. Please note, however, that all quotations are taken from the Gabler text and are not coincidental in all respects to the Random House 1961 text.

Preface

᭞Few devotees of Joyce would deny that his last two major works, *Ulysses* and *Finnegans Wake*, could be justly characterized as having comic attributes. In particular, the *Wake*, through linguistic incongruities, parody, and general tone and demeanor, is first of all a hilarious celebration of life. *Ulysses* is a more problematical book in this regard, since many of its readers and commentators over the years have described its dilemmas, its ambiguities, its lack of definitive answers as ultimately posing some of the darkest existential problems facing modern man. Carl Jung's initial reaction to *Ulysses* began an early and growing tendency among psychological critics to emphasize the dark side of the novel: "Everything is desouled, every particle of warm blood has been chilled, events unroll in icy egoism. In all the book there is nothing pleasing, nothing refreshing, nothing hopeful, but only things that are grey, grisly, gruesome, or pathetic, tragic, ironic, all from the seamy side of life and so chaotic that you have to look for thematic connections with a magnifying glass."[1]

As Jung continues to express his indignation at his own failure to understand the book, he shifts his tack to ascribing what he perceives as formlessness to what he regards as deficiencies in Joyce's own life:

> And yet they [themes] are there, first of all in the form of unavowed resentments of a highly personal nature, the wreckage of a violently amputated boyhood; then as flotsam from the whole history of thought exhibited in pitiful nakedness to the staring crowd. The religious, erotic, and domestic prehistory of the author is reflected in the drab surface of the stream of events; we even behold the disintegration of his personality into Bloom, *l'homme moyen sensuel*, and the almost gaseous Stephen Dedalus, who is mere speculation and mere mind. Of these two, the former has no son and the latter no father.[2]

It was to counter these perceived fearsome psychoanalytical aspects of the novel and to allay the charges of formlessness that Stuart Gilbert claims he wrote his early study: "Moreover, in those early days most readers and many eminent critics regarded *Ulysses* as a violently romantic work, an 'uncontrolled outpouring of the subconscious mind, powerful but formless."[3]

Still, Jung's ideas persist in more modern criticism. Among recent critics, for example, Darcy O'Brien sees the humor of *Ulysses* as masking Joyce's attempt to expunge the misery of his own sexual life:

> Although the sexual themes are more explicit in *Ulysses* than in the earlier works, Joyce disguised the close relationship between himself and his fictional character by making Bloom a Jew and a cuckold and by treating him with outrageous humor. Joyce had many reasons for giving Bloom the characteristics he did, but psychologically he needed to place Bloom at a certain distance. In this way Joyce could more easily release and give form to his observations and judgments about perverse and unhappy aspects of his sexual life.[4]

Eventually the pervasive effects of psychoanalytical revelations of the dark side of human nature in *Ulysses* gave way to expressions of modernist pessimism, such as that voiced in Robert Adams's influential *James Joyce: Common Sense and Beyond:* "The cosmos of *Ulysses* may very well prove, in the long run, exhaustible. It is a hollow world which the book presents, darker and more brittle than any which English fiction from Fielding to Hardy generally gives us." In his final evaluation of the novel, Adams goes so far as to see the book as indicative of the attitudes that produced World War II: "*Ulysses,* in 1922, described a shape of existence, a spiritual state which I recognize as culminating in 1939."[5]

Even as astute a critic as Cheryl Herr notes that what readers initially find in *Ulysses* is serious stuff indeed, especially when they translate it into the grim terms of tragedy and despair:

> At first, the reader finds in *Ulysses* the grand themes of Western literature: the son's search for the father, the father's search for the child he can never truly know to be his offspring, the artist's struggle for recognition and cash, the quest for romantic love, the often unsatisfying domestication of that love, the acceptance of death, the human battle with betrayal and despair. Visiting Ireland, the same reader may become convinced that the narrative must be understood in context: it is a book about a writer's vexed relationship to a land plagued with poverty, dominated by an oppressive foreign government, and hostile to its own prophets.[6]

In the last few years contemporary critical theorists have not so much objected to the characterization of *Ulysses* as a comic novel, as they have tended to ignore the implications of Joyce's comedy in their analysis of matters such as the relationships among meaning, text, and reader. Such criticism, profoundly il luminating as I believe it to be, is, as any theorist would admit, also the product of its age. In the present study, I do not wish to quarrel with critics whose focus is different from mine, but to reaffirm what William York Tindall said nearly forty years ago: "If the eighteenth century, supposedly the age of wit, found Swift and Sterne too witty, the plight of Joyce in our age was more desperate. Never needing the assurance of a crowd, he stood apart from those who are not only solemn but serious about it. Yet, like Shaw, Joyce was most serious and most profound when at his gayest. His humor is the proof of understanding and the sign of equanimity."[7]

Most of the negative pictures that critics derive from *Ulysses* stem from their interpretation of the basic philosophy or lack of one underlying the book. In a sense they have confused the novel's lack of a traditionally tragic moral purpose with their even grimmer view that the absence of a lofty moral direction implies that Joyce abandoned any hope of the generally pleasant sentience that life affords. It will be my contention that *Ulysses*, by embracing a more realistic comic philosophy, eschews the pretenses of the high moral dilemmas of tragedy for the normal never-ending problems of everyday life, which occur in a cycle that is as rewarding and triumphal as it is frustrating. I hope to show that, drawing its roots from antique origins and comic traditions, *Ulysses* celebrates rather than suffers life.

The five chapters in this study each attempt through a different approach to the subject of comedy to identify *Ulysses* as principally comic in design, intent, and execution. I do not mean by this to deny the validity of serious intent in such an encyclopedic work, but rather to establish that first of all Joyce's novel produces laughter, and in doing so follows a long, glorious, and purposefully dishonorable tradition.

The first chapter employs Suzanne Langer's biological-cultural approach to comedy in terms of natural philosophy. My argument treats Langer's essay as a lens through which to view the characters, motivation, language, and structure of *Ulysses*. The second chapter explores the history and theory of comedy as the oldest, most fundamental literary form, one in which the mature Joyce exercised his literary genius most profitably. I try to deal with ways in which the major treatises on the subject, including the hypothetical reconstructions of an Aristotelian Poetics of Comedy, delineate the comic character of Joyce's novel.

The third chapter deals with the central issue of linguistic parody and its comic implications, particularly for the second half of *Ulysses,* and the fourth chapter treats comic themes, characters, and techniques that Joyce shared with Rabelais, Cervantes, and Sterne. The concluding chapter emphasizes the role of the reader in determining what is or is not comic, and how comparisons and parallels from serious works such as the *Divine Comedy* can infuse comic meaning into *Ulysses*.

My attempt is, then, to deal with theory, history, and influences (past and present), in making the case that *Ulysses* is primarily a comic novel. The argument only touches briefly upon or omits much of what might profitably be further elaborated. Besides reminding the reader of something that needs to be stated, what value I hope this study has lies in its delineating the scope and potential of Joyce's comic genius.

ZACK BOWEN

Coral Gables, Florida
February 1989

Irish Studies presents a wide range of books interpreting important aspects of Irish life and culture to scholarly and general audiences. Irish literature is a special concern in the series, but works from the perspectives of the fine arts, history, and the social sciences are also welcome, as are studies which take multidisciplinary approaches.

Acknowledgments

I am indebted to Bernard Benstock, Patrick McCarthy, Mel Friedman, and particularly Frank Palmeri, Elliot Gose, Lindsey Tucker, and Claire Culleton for reading sections of my manuscript and providing invaluable advice.

A Biological
and Cultural Approach

It has always bothered me that such a funny and rewarding book as *Ulysses,* a work that ends with the resounding affirmation, "Yes," should be seen as an embodiment of hopelessness by so many, when to others like myself it represents a comic affirmation of the spirit of life. I certainly do not claim to be in any way pioneering the notion that *Ulysses* is primarily a comic novel. Richard Ellmann has always taken it for granted. His *Ulysses on the Liffey* begins: "That he [Joyce] should have written *Ulysses* as a comedy went back to a decision of early youth. He had made some effort to write tragedy in the manner of Ibsen, but concluded that comedy was his true mode. He liked comedy both in its larger sense of negotiating the reconciliation of forces, and in its more immediate sense of provoking laughter."[1] Neither do I mean to imply by my association of comedy and affirmation that comic genres such as contemporary black humor or Swiftian satire are often not essentially as grim and occasionally tragic as the plays referred to in the surviving parts of the *Poetics.* I will try to demonstrate however, that *Ulysses* is in the mainstream of comedy, which provides the vital life force of the novel. I realize that such a term as *vital life force* needs some explanation, and I would like to devote this intro-

1

duction to providing a few relevant definitions by examining Suzanne K. Langer's brilliant essay, "The Comic Rhythm," and the relationship between *Ulysses* and her extraordinary insights into art and human sensibility.[2]

Langer sees comedy as reflecting a basic biological pattern of life, or life rhythm, which when disrupted tries to restore itself and the natural balance of existence. Her examples of a tree growing taller in the shade and a fish assuming new functions with its other fins when part of its tail is bitten off are representative of biological life being confronted by obstacles and attempting to restore a balance, the process reflecting the vitality of life itself. Langer joins Francis Cornford in associating comedy with renewal and its attendant religious rites that celebrate the bringing of life into balance and in emphasizing the rhythm of sheer vitality which makes comedy its happy secret.[3] In the same way the comic novel depicts conflicts or dilemmas, resulting from accidents of fate or man's perversions and the attempt at restoring a social, biological, or psychological balance. This restoration of a balance or revivification, so closely associated with spring, plays no small part in *Ulysses*.

Beginning with the choice of a date linked with the summer solstice and a new beginning with Nora, Joyce has constructed a novel that has as one of its central propositions the conflict between men and women. This subject, according to Langer, is the greatest and perhaps sole subject of comedy because it is the most universal, human, civilized, primitive, and joyful challenge to our existence—self-preservation and self-assertion, whose progress is the comic rhythm. Women are, of course, also at the center of great tragedy: such characters as Jocasta, Gertrude, and perhaps even May Dedalus are to their male counterparts sources of ambivalent messages representing love, sin, and truth. Contests between the sexes, however, have an attitude of joyful, regenerative sexuality, which is part of the vitality of life. Stephen, as the would-be tragic figure of *Ulysses*, initially sees women as disruptive, as in their role in *Oedipus* and *Hamlet*. Representing sources of sin and guilt, even though passive, they are linked somehow with the temptress of his villanelle. Bloom, the comic center of the novel, is, in fact, engaged in a classic comic contest with Molly, the ultimate affirmation of the vital continuity that Langer calls the comic spirit. Molly is both antagonistic to and affirmative of Bloom's efforts and life. It is Molly's soliloquy in Penelope that finally confirms the fact that the obstacles facing Bloom are all trivial, and she becomes spokesperson for the ultimate common sense that is the hallmark of comedy. Unlike tragedy, the agon of comedy, including *Ulysses,* embraces a struggle of words: debates, arguments, and catechisms which mock tragic moral struggle. Molly's soliloquy is but the final expression of this parody. We shall examine this aspect of comedy in detail in the chapter on narration.

We shall also see that the aspects of the tragic impulse that do exist in *Ulysses* are relegated to the still-undeveloped Stephen; his is the moral struggle with the past, with the guilt over his mother, with the great choices of whether to assume the sins of his country and lead his people messianically out of bondage. But the tragic spirit is inimical to the comic hero, because comic characters have a morality which is complete, in the sense that their principles are generally clear and coherent enough so that they do not face soul-wrenching moral decisions. Thus, Langer suggests, the action in comedies derives from the changes of fortune that the comic heroes encounter. Leopold Bloom, from his first discourses with the cat in Calypso through his final reflections in Ithaca, is the ultimate comic hero. His challenges derive from obstacles such as Blazes Boylan on the path of Bloom's marital bliss, and from his failure to bring about societal changes through his schemes for such political and social benefits as communal kitchens and endowments for infants, and ultimately from his seeming inability to appear as a heroic figure to his wife. While Stephen is still engaged in a great search for a moral blueprint for his place in the universe, Bloom proceeds with moral certitude into the void. He will meet his misfortunes with reason, the highest virtue of the human soul, and in a sense emerge victoriously, still combative in a struggle that will never be resolved and for which no ultimate victory is possible.

Thus, even Stephen's position as would-be tragic hero in a *bildungsroman* search for his personal truth, which initially sets the tone and direction of the novel as a potentially tragic and solemn work, must give way to the mundane certitudes and rationality of the central comic figure, Leopold Bloom. In the past Stephen has sought an intellectual answer to his moral dilemmas in an attempt to reconcile the artist and his work to the psychological and physical changes in his environment. His past, bound up in allusions which display a Catholic sense of guilt over sins relating to religion, country, and family, has led Stephen to seek an amoral philosophy in an art detached from its maker and outside of the moral or political spheres. This nondidactic truth, which Stephen calls "dramatic," is the kind that can only be found in comedy. Thus, by the time Stephen reaches the state of mind that embraces his new Shakespearean aesthetic theory in *Ulysses,* the relationship of artist to art (of Shakespeare's writing *Hamlet* to free himself of his own personal feelings regarding his cuckolding wife) has become in a sense trivialized by reason.

The flippant tone of the narration which mirrors Stephen's attitudes in Scylla and Stephen's admission that he doesn't believe his own theory indicate his realization that his associating his own plight with Hamlet's and ultimately Shakespeare's has become more comic than tragic. The forced parallels and altered facts in his presentation to the librarian's company in Scylla begin, for the first time in *Ulysses,* to take on more comic than tragic overtones.

The comic antidote for Stephen's self-generated dilemma is Bloom's quiet certitude. The latter's comic, often zany, upsidedown way of looking at both life and Molly's rump; his enjoyment of life's vital processes of ingestion and elimination; his ever-present, oft-thwarted sexual drives; his sexual surrogates of ladies' ankles, knickers, and other fetishistic garments and activities; and his pleasant, calm acceptance of masturbation as a substitute for coition are all like Langer's damaged fish who navigates as nearly as possible with the remaining pectorals and dorsals at its disposal in an attempt to restore nature's balance. If Bloom can't take satisfaction in either traditional societal approbation or financial remuneration for his talent, and if he is no longer the sole or even infrequent proprietor of Molly's body, he nevertheless follows the comic tradition by achieving a measure of satisfaction from his own, more basic bodily functions such as taste, flatulence, and elimination. He derives sensual pleasure not only from self-manipulation but from a host of fetishistic female surrogates. In doing so Bloom has in a serious but comic way become more independent, more able to survive in the often inhospitable environs of dear dirty Dublin.

While Stephen's all-encompassing theories about life and art and *Hamlet* are trivialized in the library scene, Bloom's mundane philosophy and rationality gain importance as natural functions of survival and vitality for the common man. The pretensions of Stephen's vision cannot stand the light of comic reality because they lack vitality, whereas although Bloom's unique if zany solutions to both his and society's problems seem ridiculous, they nevertheless possess the vital energy that transcends traditional morality and informs a comic vision that reduces the greatest epic in Western civilization to a set of domestic circumstances.

The absurdity of the whole idea of Ithaca on Eccles Street, with its comic logic, provides the sense that the epic, the past recapitulated in contemporary life, need not be tragic or dark. If, like our undistinguished hero, Bloom, we are not carried away with self-importance, the very paradox of reliving Odysseus's adventures every day provides its own comic salvation. Such conjunctions as citizen and Cyclops spring from a comic source that enables us to carry on, to see things in common terms, which, in fact, are more characteristic of our daily life than the tragic scenarios we sometimes project on to it. Our fear of apocalypses as yet unsuffered—our tendency to aggrandize our condition into artistic cosmic and tragic terms—when mitigated by a comic rationality and a sense of where we are, is rendered laughable by the welter of the mundane things that comprise the vitality of life. *Ulysses* reaffirms that sense of comic process.

The novel abounds in testimony to the comic view of life. Trivializing the grand and aggrandizing the trivial are a part of the comic tradition. Joyce, the consummate self-reflexive artist, caricatures himself in Stephen Dedalus, and invites further self-comparison with the modern ineffectual epic hero, Leopold Bloom. In doing so, Joyce abandons the tragic mode, because his artistic protagonist ceases to loom larger than life and becomes another comic character living through the trivia of contemporary detail. The reader is left with the paradoxical impression that the everyman in each of us is vital and unique, that the trivial aspects are in fact more rationally and meaningfully heroic than the rantings of tragic heroes caught in self-inflicted moral dilemmas.

The audience, lulled into a sense of comic detachment by the possibility that neither Bloom nor Stephen is more noble than they, fails initially to identify with either character. It is one of the great ironies of the comic situation that comedy, with its attention to the common aspects of daily life, really inspires an even closer ultimate identification than the audience feels with its tragic heroes, an identification that we consciously shun, but unconsciously accept. Thus, when we laugh at the hero's plight and his fumblings, we are assured — without realizing that we harbor any pity and fear for the hero—that our own problems are universal, that we are at least as able to cope with them as the hero, and finally, that a satisfactory struggle has in itself a measure of sufficiency no matter how badly we bumble our attempts at solutions.

If Bloom can be a hero, inviting comparison with Ulysses, then so can we all. If Bloom's life is not so horrible, if his sense of equanimity, his inability to realize that he has lost, somehow makes his ignorance a triumph, it assures us that we, who are as good as he, might experience something of the same. At the end of the novel Stephen's plight is not resolved anymore than is Bloom's. Comedies do not bring ultimate solutions to life; they depict the vitality in the ongoing struggle.

None of this is meant to imply that Bloom is wholly a buffoon; he is a rational, sensitive, compassionate, humane man. There is so much good about Bloom that an identification with him assures us that we ourselves are better. Such an association is a reversed, comic version of Aristotle's *Poetics* dictum that the audience identify with a protagonist of higher social status. In comedy the reverse is true: we identify with a protagonist of equal or lower fortune, who possesses either dubious or greater moral courage than the audience. If Bloom learns nothing, no moral answers from the day's dilemmas, we are assured that because the answers have not come to us, we are no more lost than he. If he wants to feel an identification with the past and the future, then so do we. Like Aeneas leaving burning Troy with his father on his back, his son at his side, we want to be assured of a continuity. That continuity, a source of the comic vitality Langer speaks of, is represented in a number of ways in *Ulysses*, but it is no more apparent than in the father-son theme.

Stephen, like Telemachus, sets out in search of a father figure. While a great deal of philosophical speculation among *Ulysses* critics turns on whether Bloom fulfills the role as Stephen's spiritual father, Bloom, unlike his putative offspring, is searching for a flesh-and-blood son to replace the dead Rudy. Stephen, on the other hand, already has a real father, Simon Dedalus, a character we see several times during the day, much to our delight, for Simon is a funny man. His aphorisms, his clichés, his exaggerated and comic sense of his own tragic dilemmas, his bombastic railing at his in-laws, and his generally lackadaisical attitude regarding the financial and spiritual support of his family are but a few of the delights that make Simon a classic comic character. Stephen's perhaps subconscious and certainly grudging respect for his father's comic presence is manifested in Proteus, when Stephen recites nearly word for word an entire litany of Simon's traditional ridicule of his in-laws. We learn the accuracy of Stephen's mimicry later when we hear nearly the same words from Simon's own lips. While his comedy is often at others' expense, his own figure is the object of satire. Whether Stephen approves or not, Simon's excuses, his bombast, his Macawber-like character provide his son with a sense of the comic, the ironic, and the incongruous in life. For Stephen, Simon is certainly no tragic hero wrestling with great moral dilemmas, and consequently Stephen's understanding of his father's shortcomings brings him a great deal closer to accepting the mundane comedy of a father like Bloom than Stephen consciously knows.

The other examples of paternity which augment the central triangle of Simon, Stephen, and Bloom are the *Hamlet* and Holy Trinity motifs on one side and such mundane domestic pairings as Paddy Dignam and son, Reuben J. Dodd and son, and D. B. Murphy and son on the other. The latter all have comic associations. Reuben J. Dodd and son are the subjects of a joke about the elder Dodd giving the boatman who pulled Dodd's suicidal offspring from the river a florin for the rescue. The anecdote is started by Leopold Bloom and finished by the Shakespeare-father-surrogate, Martin Cunningham, while they are on the way to Dignam's funeral, accompanied by Simon Dedalus, whose genuinely funny line, "One and eightpence too much," completes the Dodd story. In another comic variation on the paternal motif, the entire company is seated upon sperm-stained seats, the result of lovemaking in the funeral carriage. The comic incongruity underscores Langer's basic linking of comedy with survival. Like most of the essentially comic events, the atmosphere, as Bloom speculates, represents life or vitality in the midst of death.

D. B. Murphy, one of the great comic characters of modern literature, is another Ulysses-Sinbad traveler with a runaway son, Danny, who left a draper's shop in Cork for a life at sea. Murphy's comic and highly dubious accounts of his own adventures parallel the Odyssean motif and regale both would-be father and son. His comic vitality and the artistry of his fabrications rival those of Odysseus and underscore the link between the paternal theme and artistic creation, especially when Murphy claims to know Simon personally and then tells a completely phony story about Simon's marksmanship in the Hengler circus in Stockholm.

Bloom's father's suicide, certainly not a comic theme, is overshadowed by Bloom's attachment to the past through his grandfather, Lipoti Virag, whose id in Circe projects a vigorous sensuality in the form of a funny libidinous impulse toward women and sex. He is the patriarchal counterpart to Stephen's paternal predecessor, Simon Dedalus. Fathers and grandfathers, it seems, provide a basis for coping with reality rather than with spiritual dilemmas. They are the mundane Panza figures whose low roads to life supply the comic vitality necessary to survive.

Stephen's initial vision furnishes the framework of the novel, much as his Odyssean counterpart, Telemachus, pervades the medias res beginning of the *Odyssey* and forms our expectations of what his father may eventually do. Stephen becomes the architect of *Ulysses,* shaping our expectations of what his father-surrogate might be like, the manner in which Stephen will meet him, and the sort of relationship they will eventually establish. In the comic world of *Ulysses,* however, nothing is resolved. The action of the novel is incomplete and ongoing, an experience of the vital continuity of life rather than the complete action of an *Odyssey*. Bloom never assumes complete control, the action is not finished, and the continuity between father and son is subsumed into the greater continuity of events in the everyday world of *Ulysses*.

The comic universe is defined by senseless turns of events transformed by artistry into a sort of drollery, a world where the plights of the characters invite instant, everyday identification and where the crude and the sublime exist side by side. In the chapter on comic predecessors we shall examine how in *Ulysses*, Bloom-Panza provides the comic counterpart to most of Stephen-Quixote's serious, high-artistic vision. In counterpoint to Stephen's deification of art, Bloom's own artistic ventures are of a much lower order. The conjunction of the artwork "Matcham's Masterstroke" and Bloom's own artistic production of a turd "just right . . . quick and neat" (*U* 4:510, 511 – 12; 1961:69) is confirmed by Bloom's use of the prize titbit as toilet paper. Lest we missed it, the connection is underscored again in Circe with Beaufoy's exhibiting "a specimen of my maturer work disfigured by the hallmark of the beast" (*U* 15:844 – 45; 1961:459). Later, in the comic narrative chapter, we shall explore the allied proposition that Bloom's aspirations as an artist writing his experiences in a cabman's shelter are comic projections of Stephen's own ambitions and perhaps even Joyce's in writing Eumaeus.

Buck Mulligan joins Bloom in debunking the artistic visions of Stephen Dedalus; Mulligan uses irony, satire, and wit in his parodies of Stephen as priest in the beginning, of Dedalus-Christ as artist in "The Ballad of Joking Jesus," and of Stephen as self-reflexive artist in Mulligan's masturbatory version of *Hamlet*. However, Bloom's commentary, which he never intended to be a didactic satire on another's work, is a more constructive reduction of the artistic impulse to a lower common denominator of comedy. He will not ask for much from his son-surrogate Stephen — perhaps a chance to make a little money from the joint concert tours of his newfound progeny and his wife. It does not cross Bloom's mind that he could be either subject or object of any potential literary artistry, although as incestuous mother-surrogate, Molly, during her Penelope musings, certainly envisions her role as a sexual inspiration figure. The last conjunction between the would-be father and would-be artist son is manifested in the crossing of the trajectories of their urinations, a final ironic and genuinely funny comment on their aspirations.

Bloom also fits the traditional comic picture of the spiritual misfit. From Dogberry to Lucky Jim, comedy has long embraced the concept of the person who simply does not fit into a traditional spiritual-theological system. While his own misfit role is a source of anguish for Stephen, Bloom comfortably looks at the church's power, money, and ludicrousness from a healthy sense of commonplace agnosticism. Bloom is a quasi-Protestant, Catholic, and Jew, fitting no creed and untutored in all, except for bits and pieces of Hebraic lore. There is just enough earthy Jewishness in Bloom to cast him as a *schlemiel* figure, the traditional comic Jewish masochist, an intelligent yet chronically mistake-making creature who revels in his misery. *Ulysses* is tinged with this bit of ethnic humor, but it is only a part of Bloom's multifaceted makeup. As spiritual misfit, Bloom embodies the traditional comic salvation of the powerless against the powerful, the individual against the social order. He operates outside of the traditional conventions of religion by seeking as much as possible between the natural poles of birth and death. The vitality of this philosophy embodies his natural religion, so closely akin to the comic spirit. While religion, like tragedy, depends upon the fatalistic, comedy, exemplified by Bloom's approach to religion and the rest of his life, depends upon fortune. He reacts to events as they occur. His life, therefore, is essentially contingent, episodic, and ethnic, the very hallmarks of comedy as outlined by Langer. His schemes for tram lines to the cemetery and social reform are part of both his Jewish and Irish heritage, and his search for a son to replace Rudy is inextricably linked to his Semitic background. His chance meetings with Stephen, coincidental with the birth of Mina Purefoy and the *Hamlet* aesthetic highjinks in the library, are used by Bloom to develop a relationship which spans but a few hours of his life, in a day largely dependent upon such transitory factors as place, time, social conventions, and Bloom's ethnicity as both Irishman and Jew.

Social convention and constraints play a far larger part in comedy than they do in tragedy. Because the characters in a comedy are part of a vital continuity, they are a part of life as it exists rather than being the reshapers or changers that tragic heroes are. Comic characters, like the fish and the tree, adapt to existing circumstances and do not affect large changes in the social order. The comic hero's enemy is an uncongenial world to which he shapes or adapts his own fortune. Thus, if *Ulysses* were indeed a comedy, one would not expect the cosmos of Dublin and environs to be radically changed or reshaped. The lack of purposeful action oft cited by early critics would be a flaw in a tragic novel, but it is the norm in a comic. As readers of a tragic *Ulysses* we hope to impart dramatic import into such trivia as who will get whose breakfast the next morning. But the very ludicrousness of the breakfast question as an answer to tragic problems is funny in itself. Of course nothing much is changed. The question is how Bloom and Stephen cope with existing circumstances and how they change or adapt themselves to meet those circumstances.

Once we have established the comic intent of *Ulysses*, the other features of comedy embodied in the book become apparent. As Langer points out, the laughter in comedy comes about as a result of the totality of the action. Having established itself in a comic milieu, each individual scene produces laughter not merely because it is indigenously funny in itself, but because it is a part of the entire comic action of the work, so that, for instance, Molly's memory of Bloom's suggestion about milking her breasts into his tea in the morning, a mild joke in itself, produces a disproportionate laughter because it is a general part of Bloom's entire comic personality. When we laugh at acts such as Murphy's emptying his bilge beside the cabman's shelter, we are laughing at the whole novel and not merely at the immediate action. Comedy sustains itself through its individual elements, and as the audience's awareness of the comic sensibility heightens, each individual comic incident becomes funnier, rather than merely tragically ironic. Thus the final *Yes*, translated by unimaginative or pessimistic critics into *No*, becomes anomalous if it is not an affirmation of life's comic vitality.

Of course it is not merely a string of situations that maintain the comic atmosphere of the novel, but Joyce's whole plethora of comic, particularly linguistic, devices. (We will treat these devices at length in the narration chapter.) On the first page Joyce commences with ribald parody, burlesque, and blasphemy to destroy the seriousness and potential tragedy of Stephen's outlook, and continues with increasingly comic linguistic acrobatics from the headlines in the Aeolus chapter, through the Gregorian notation of Scylla, to the musical-comedy world of Dublin in song in Sirens.

As the narration itself shifts gears, the comedy increases in Cyclops, with its mundane barfly and hyperbolizing narrators jointly trivializing or magnifying to the point of ridiculousness. The meanness of the barfly's and citizen's points of view, counterpointed by the aggrandizements of the omniscient narrator, are all to be seen in contrast to Bloom's doctrine of love and his humanitarian efforts on behalf of the Dignams. The ineffectuality of the last hyperbolized exchange between Bloom and the citizen completes the comic scene. Joyce leads us on a merry chase from the parodies of the mundane literature framing the thoughts of an adolescent Dublin girl, through the grotesque twistings and turnings of a series of opinionated period narrators in Oxen of the Sun, through the farce of Circe — in which the libido itself is objectified in all its drollery—and through the cliché-ridden half-truths and vitality of Eumaeus to our final nonanswers in catechism and science in Ithaca, followed by the culminating comic Gea-Tellus omniscience of the earthy Molly.

The linguistic devices aggrandize the mundane. The Irish hyperbole of describing Bloom as Elijah ascending "at an angle of fortyfive degrees over Donohoe's in Little Green street like a shot off a shovel" (*U* 12:1917–18; 1961:345) is typical. The great comic technique of *Ulysses* is that the actions which seem to appear so important, and hence serious, are made trivial by aggrandizement. Joyce's long discourse on the trifling contents of a drawer in Bloom's house, the elaborate elucidation of Bloom's fantasies in Circe, Gerty McDowell's fashioning Bloom's masturbation into a classic romantic moment — all are indicative of the length to which comedy goes to render normal activities even more trivial by aggrandizing them. At the same time, the reader is left with a feeling for the genuine vitality of the common and a sense that life's continuity and vitality have been reestablished. The unrealistic epic proportions to which Joyce takes the action through his linguistic parodies restore balance by emphasizing the importance of the trivial which remains at the core of existence. The whole idea of the Odyssean epic of Eccles Street itself assumes greater comic tone with each new outlandish linguistic feat, each new mundane circumstance made artificially important, increasing our laughter at the totality of the comic experience.

Langer admonishes that comedy must guard against "any backsliding into the world of anxious interest and selfish solicitude."[4] The comic art in essence represents a generalization about life's mundane complications without arousing the terror of tragedy. We are to be reminded that we are witnessing an amusing artifice, although its ultimate truth is universal. Joyce accomplishes this goal by use of such devices as varying his narrative methods and by the absurdity of the coincidences and crisscrossing of motifs and meanings. If we ever tend to forget that *Ulysses* is a funny book, we need only refer to the comic innovations and devices of Joyce's style, his scores of variations on established motifs and themes, until at last its protagonist becomes the symbol of the vital continuity of life, never destroyed, if momentarily defeated, as nature and process go on. Whatever Molly's "Yes" signifies, it is, as Langer points out, the final aspect of the comic spirit, because vital continuity begets affirmation of process rather than ultimate answers. As Langer sums up her chapter on comedy, "Not the derivation of personages and situations, but of the rhythm of 'felt life' that the poet puts upon them, seems to me to be of artistic importance: the essential comic feeling, which is the sentient aspect of organic unity, growth, and self-preservation."[5]

The reader leaves *Ulysses* with the idea that Bloom and Molly's existence will continue with the same vitality and urgency. If the book provided ultimate answers to their problems, the vitality would be less than realistic; we are left instead with the more fundamental comic assertion that life goes on.

Ulysses and Comic Theory

The relationship between comedy and ancient ritual has been explored and redefined in the twentieth century, first by Francis Cornford, who in 1914, when Joyce was beginning to compose his ideas for *Ulysses*, developed Frazer's theory of religious rituals into his widely read *The Origin of Attic Comedy*, a milestone in our understanding of the evolution of Greek, and subsequently Western, comic tradition. Cornford argued, in his now universally accepted thesis, that the seasonal conflict between winter and summer, death and resurrection, in the annual vegetation cycle provided the basis for the comedy of the early folk festivals, which in turn were the forerunners of the classic Athenian Dionysian comedies.

The phallic processions that signaled the early rustic events connected human reproduction with the reproductive cycle associated with the passing of winter and the inevitable cycle of life. Mikhail Bakhtin has traced their recurrence through medieval carnivals and processions and into the works of Rabelais and Cervantes. Bakhtin describes a culture of folk humor:

And yet, the scope and the importance of this culture were immense in the Renaissance and the Middle Ages. A boundless world of humorous forms and manifestations opposed the official and serious tone of medieval ecclesiastical and feudal culture. In spite of their variety, folk festivals of the carnival type, the comic rites and cults, the clowns and fools, giants, dwarfs, and jugglers, the vast and manifold literature of parody — all these forms have one style in common: they belong to one culture of folk carnival humor.[1]

The carnivals were free from religious mysticism and piety, which led to "the creation of special forms of marketplace speech and gesture, frank and free, permitting no distance between those who came in contact with each other and liberating from norms of etiquette and decency imposed at other times."[2]

Ulysses operates squarely in this comic tradition. Not only is it egalitarian in its choice of protagonist and in its commonality of situation, but its language and activities so often hark back to the carnivalistic that Joyce was early and often, like his comic predecessors, accused of obscenity and of trafficking in filth and degradation. Bakhtin defends their presence in modern literature:

it would be absurd and hypocritical to deny the attraction which these expressions still exercise even when they are without erotic connotation. A vague memory of past carnival liberties and carnival truth still slumbers in these modern forms of abuse. The problem of their irrepressible linguistic vitality has as yet not been seriously posed. In the age of Rabelais abuses and curses still retained their full meaning in the popular language from which his novel sprang, and above all they retained their positive, regenerating pole.[3]

We will explore in detail in a later chapter the affinities between Joyce and Rabelais, and how their comic approach is similarly regenerative.

Bakhtin traces the development of the grotesque to the carnivalistic comic strain, which is also so apparent in Joyce:

> the carnival-grotesque form exercises the same function: to consecrate inventive freedom, to permit the combination of a variety of different elements and their rapprochement, to liberate from the prevailing point of view of the world, from conventions and established truths, from clichés, from all that is humdrum and universally accepted. This carnival spirit offers the chance to have a new outlook on the world, to realize the relative nature of all that exists, and to enter a completely new order of things.[4]

Circe is the prime example of exactly that grotesquerie. It is difficult to understand why this episode has not always been universally viewed as comedic. Some of the funniest scenes in literature appear there, and from the stage directions introducing the chapter, the chapter appears to defy realistic, that is, established, credibility. But Circe has been so tarred with the brush of the terrifying aspects of the subliminal that critics, since Mark Shechner at least, have tended to treat it as serious stuff indeed.[5] Bakhtin would classify the episode with the romantic grotesque, which still retains the laughter of a carnival spirit that strips the terrifying (demons, and so forth) of its dreadful aspects. The heavy emphasis on sex in Circe is more comforting than disconcerting because it underlies the comic regenerative force in a natural cycle that sees the grotesque as a part of a new and joyous beginning. Since much of the overt sexuality and the prominence of bodily functions in comedy have roots older than tragedy's character flaws, it is no accident that the three comic predecessors of Joyce who are discussed in this book have all, like Joyce, represented the bodily functions of daily living that are virtually ignored in tragedy and in serious fiction.

Scholars of the comic tradition agree that the events comedy portrays are those of everyday existence, because, as Cornford observed, comedy seeks to portray characters in universal rather than in unique situations.[6] Hence comedy is far less subservient to the dictates of plot than it is to character. Another aspect of comedy, evolving from the universal participation of medieval townspeople in the carnival celebrations, is that hierarchical precedence is suspended into a universal equality with high and low equally represented by occupation.[7] From phallic processions to puppet shows, comedy evolved a stock set of characters who were much more dependent on ritual situations than the momentous soul-searching activities of tragedy's superior protagonists would allow. Hence comedy remained closer to its ritualistic cyclical origins.

If Joyce indeed set out to write a comic novel, he certainly afforded it a ritualistic background right from the first page, on which Buck Mulligan comically intones the beginning of the Mass, a contemporary survival of the old fertility myths of resurrection and regeneration. After a brief conversation with the cat, whose mythic origins I will not pursue, Bloom begins his activities with a walk in the sun on a June day less than a week before the summer solstice. After establishing his credentials as a talisman-bearing wanderer by confirming the absence of his key and the presence of his potato, Bloom immediately senses the reassuring presence of the sun:

> The sun was nearing the steeple of George's church. Be a warm day I fancy. Specially in these black clothes feel it more.

> Black conducts, reflects, (refracts is it?), the heat. But I couldn't go in that light suit. Make a picnic of it. His eyelids sank quietly often as he walked in happy warmth. Boland's breadvan delivering with trays our daily but she prefers yesterday's loaves turnovers crisp crowns hot. Makes you feel young. Somewhere in the east: early morning: set off at dawn. Travel round in front of the sun, steal a day's march on him. Keep it up for ever never grow a day older technically. (*U* 4:78–86; 1961:57)

This remarkable passage precedes Bloom's vision of himself wandering through the Middle East. He is cheered by the new-born sun, though it will create some discomfort because he is dressed in black for death, Dignam's funeral. The warm sun of the late spring morning is his saving grace. As he passes the breadvan, he translates the contents into ritual terms by a gratuitous reference to the Lord's Prayer. The perpetual rising of the sun in the east triggers a Bloomian vision of achieving an endless cycle of eternal youth by staying just ahead of the ever-rising, never-dying sun as it circles the globe, technically never getting a day older. Bloom's idea contrasts with Ireland's home-rule sun, doomed from its inception by rising on the wrong side.

After he comes out of Dlugacz's with his ritual kidney, his thoughts are again solar-shaped, this time by the absence of the sun's rays:

> A cloud began to cover the sun slowly, wholly. Grey. Far. No, not like that. A barren land, bare waste. Vulcanic lake, the dead sea: no fish, weedless, sunk deep in the earth. No wind could lift those waves, grey metal, poisonous foggy waters. Brimstone they called it raining down: the cities of the plain: Sodom, Gomorrah, Edom. All dead names. A dead sea in a dead land, grey and old. Old now. It bore the oldest, the

first race. A bent hag crossed from Cassidy's, clutching a nag-
gin bottle by the neck. The oldest people. Wandered far away
over all the earth, captivity to captivity, multiplying, dying,
being born everywhere. It lay there now. Now it could bear no
more. Dead: an old woman's: the grey sunken cunt of the
world.
        Desolation. (*U* 4:218–28; 1961:61)

The absence of the sun brings about thoughts of Bloom's own
race, and a comparison of their dead civilization and homeland
to Ireland. The bent hag, reminiscent of the milkwoman Stephen has recently associated with Ireland, makes her appearance in juxtaposition with Bloom's image of an exhausted female reproductive principle. This seems hardly a cheery
prospect on which to begin a comedy, but momentarily Bloom's
thoughts brighten again with the return of the sun: "Quick
warm sunlight came running from Berkeley road, swiftly, in
slim sandals, along the brightening footpath. Runs, she runs to
meet me, a girl with gold hair on the wind" (*U* 4:240 – 42;
1961:61). The old hag has been replaced by a new young girl,
and, with no transition, Bloom is back home with his consort,
Molly. At this formative stage of the novel, Joyce's obvious associations of death with regeneration and the war of the seasons is
the stuff of Attic comedy, an announcement of comic intent.
        Cornford points out that the strife between the seasons
evolved into the debates of the Greek comedies. Because the
comedies were concerned with the everyday life of the marketplace, the chorus was called upon to give voice to the debates. In
the *agon*, the duel of the adversaries was most frequently expressed by the opinions of a divided chorus, as in the choruses
of men and women in *Lysistrata*. Joyce employs these chorus
scenes of public debate and contending in innumerable scenes in
Ulysses: in the joke-telling rivalry in the funeral cab, in the rhetorical contest in the newspaper office, in the musical contest of

Sirens, in the competitive ribaldry of Oxen, in the sexual rivalry of the whores at Bella's, in the rivalry over credibility at the cabman's shelter, in the patriotic rivalry at Barney Kiernan's, and anywhere else two or three Dubliners gather on Bloomsday. The city-dwellers are part of a constant, ever-changing, comic chorus of trivia and comic debate all day long.

Like ancient comedy with its sung choruses, *Ulysses* has its music, more than 850 musical allusions during the course of the novel, many linked to their sexually-motivated predecessors, love's old sweet songs from Attica, where music forms a part of the background to the concluding preservation of the ritual marriage between the fertility king and queen. If Molly's final acceptance of Bloom is conflated with her first acceptance of Mulvey, few readers think that the Blooms' marriage is in serious jeopardy. There is too much sunshine in the conclusion of Molly's soliloquy for that: "they might as well try to stop the sun from rising tomorrow the sun shines for you he said the day we were lying among the rhododendrons on Howth head in the grey tweed suit and his straw hat the day I got him to propose to me yes first I gave him the bit of seedcake out of my mouth and it was leapyear like now yes" (*U* 18:1571–75; 1961:782). The book's ending with the ritual reestablishment of the fertility marriage (i.e., seedcake mouth to mouth) could hardly have been accidental.

By tracing the evolution of comic situations, characters, and devices through Western literature, Northrop Frye formulated an archetypal tradition where Cornford left off. In order to trace the common elements of comedy, Frye necessarily draws upon broad generalities, especially when they apply to the nature of the comic world and the lessons derived from it. Many of Frye's dicta apply directly to *Ulysses*. Among the most widely accepted is the direction that comedy takes: "The movement from *pistis* to *gnosis*, from a society controlled by habit, ritual bondage, arbitrary law and the older characters to a society controlled by youth and pragmatic freedom is fundamentally, as the Greek words suggest, a movement from illusion to reality. Illusion is whatever is fixed or definable, and reality is best understood as its negation."[8] Ironically, the source of liberating comedy in *Ulysses* is the older protagonist, Bloom, whose earthy reality acts as a comic corrective to the guilt-ridden ecclesiastical patriotism Stephen has been trying so hard to escape through his illusions of artistic freedom and aesthetic principle. The signs of the old arbitrary order surface everywhere in Dublin and its environs, and Stephen's desperate attempt to escape seems doomed. But the liberating incongruity of Bloom's humorous equanimity provides a comic antidote of mundane rebellion to the outrages of the Deasys, the Citizens, and the priests. Bloom's chaos and lack of a methodical philosophical center stand in direct opposition to Stephen's Thomistic attempts to analogize, define, and categorize. Bloom's world corresponds to what Frye describes as "a Saturnalia, a reversal of social standards which recalls a golden age in the past before the main action of the play begins."[9] Bloom and Molly indeed move to their own respective drummers.

The Saturnalia of Bloom and Molly provides a final comic picture which is predictably difficult to define, thus coinciding with Frye's definition of the classic comic society: "The society emerging at the conclusion of comedy represents ... a kind of moral norm, or pragmatically free society. Its ideals are seldom defined or formulated: definition and formulation belong to the humors, who want predictable activity."[10] The ambiguity of the conclusion of *Ulysses* is certainly due in some not inconsequential measure to the comic nature of the novel. "Living happily ever after" is a cliché a modern comic novelist would use only satirically, but surviving with humor and equanimity all of the outrages both domestic and public that life has heaped upon its practitioners is a comic conclusion indeed.

The image of the Blooms prevails at the end over the literary-artistic images and philosophical motifs of Stephen Dedalus. In the movement away from the *Portrait*-dominated systematic mind of the young artist to the hedonistic mentality of Bloom, Joyce slightly alters the usual practice of having a socially prestigious or powerful paternal figure force much of the play's society into line with his obsession. Instead Joyce gives his younger protagonist, Stephen, an irrational Quixotic twist and juxtaposes against him a figure who, like the Greek middle comedy buffoons, is connected with cooking and the satisfaction of appetites of all kinds. The first thing we learn about Bloom is his relish for the ingestion of internal organs, as he sets about preparing his breakfast. The result of the contest between the winter of Stephen's discontent and the summer of Bloom's Agendath Netaim vision is never in doubt. I suspect that once Joyce introduced Bloom, and saw the power of the figure he had created so different from himself, his sense of the predominance of the comic spirit increased with each successive chapter, until it became the prevailing mode of the novel — a juxtaposition of the realities of existence against the illusions of youth. The novel, then, exemplifies Frye's second or "Quixotic phase" of comedy, in which "the hero is usually himself at least partly a comic humor or mental runaway, and we have either a hero's illusion thwarted by a superior reality or a clash of two illusions."[11]

There is a question, of course, about whether Bloom's reality does in fact thwart Stephen's illusions, since the evidence we have is that Stephen, despite his feeling "a strange kind of flesh of a different man approach him" (*U* 16:1723 – 24; 1961:660), is not about to be subsumed into Bloom's world. The point is whether in the reader's mind Bloom's comic world has triumphed in the battle of the two opposing ideologies, and whether Stephen and Bloom are really pursuing the same set of goals through various common motifs or analogous situations. Certainly the protean aspects of transformation, addressed elsewhere in this study, lead us to parallel ideas, themes, and incidents involving Stephen and Bloom. That again, according to Frye, is a classic characteristic of comedy: "The action of comedy in moving from one social center to another is not unlike the action of a lawsuit, in which plaintiff and defendant construct different versions of the same situation, one finally being judged as real and the other as illusory. This resemblance of the rhetoric of comedy to the rhetoric of jurisprudence has been recognized from earliest times."[12] For instance, in the *Ulysses* version of one motif that Frye designates as a minor order of comedy — the frequent possibilities of incestuous combinations — Stephen's preoccupation with *Hamlet* arises in part from his interest in the theme of oedipal incest, which creeps into his agenbite of inwit, and later into his Scylla dialogue on Shakespeare. In assuming the role of a putative father in need of a son, Bloom introduces the possibility, later graphically spelled out in comic detail by Molly, of incest right there on Eccles Street. Certainly in introducing Stephen to his would-be mother through a bosomy pictorial likeness, Bloom apparently is catering to Stephen's baser instincts, a predisposition that Bloom's earlier masochism has led us to expect.

Another aspect of the transformation process is the doubling technique. Robert Alter, in discussing the proliferation of doubles in the self-conscious novel, notably *Don Quixote*, also asserts their prevalence in comedy: "A double, of course, is a reflection or imitation, and often a covertly parodistic imitation that exposes hidden aspects of the original. . . . It should be emphasized . . . that the self-conscious novelist utilizes the double with a conscious quality of intellectual playfulness, in sharp contrast to writers like Poe, Dostoevski, and Conrad, who try to give the double its full mythic resonance as an embodiment of the dark Other Side of the self."[13] The doubling aspect of comedy so pervades *Ulysses* that there is scarcely a theme or situation that does not have its low counterpart, many of which are recognized overtly as parodic and comic versions in the recapitulatory Circe episode. Doubling is one aspect of a series of thematic and linguistic repetitions. Frye discusses the comic function of such repetitions: "The principle of the humor is the principle that unincremental repetition, the literary imitation of ritual bondage, is funny.... Repetition overdone or not going anywhere belongs to comedy, for laughter is partly a reflex, and like other reflexes it can be conditioned by a simple repeated pattern."[14] As we shall see in the chapter on comic narrative, the incremental lists of names and the repeated linguistic devices serve as one kind of comic repetition, while actions and motif serve as another.

Structurally, according to Frye, "an extraordinary number of comic stories, both in drama and fiction, seem to approach a potentially tragic crisis near the end."[15] Again *Ulysses* is no exception. One such climax is the four o'clock hour of assignation, with Bloom sentimentally aroused by Simon's rendition of *"M'appari,"* and the second occurs in Ithaca, when Stephen, offered the hospitality of the Blooms, refuses. Comic narration saves both scenes from becoming "serious, sentimental, or ominous of potential catastrophe," in Frye's terminology, first, in the description of Simon's high B flat at the end of the song, and then, in Ithaca, by the irrelevant questions and answers intervening between Bloom's invitation and Stephen's answer, and finally, by the comic formality with which the response is phrased:

> Was the proposal of asylum accepted?
>
> Promptly, inexplicably, with amicability, gratefully it was declined. (*U* 17:954–55; 1961:695).

Bloom has waited all day, every day since Rudy's death for another son or at least a surrogate. He has a lot of psychic pain or pleasure riding on Stephen's response. But Joyce was not about to give any quarter from his basically comic view. Once the reader begins to feel pity and fear, the comic game is up.

Frye joins the Aristotelians in placing primary emphasis for the meaning of comedy on audience reaction, and there is more to it than simply pity and fear: "The resolution of comedy comes, so to speak, from the audience's side of the stage; in a tragedy it comes from some mysterious world on the opposite side."[16] The primary meaning of this statement is that comedy is grounded on the everyday events which are part of the audience's normal experience, rather than on cosmic higher values, but Frye's assertion also opens the door to a definition of comedy similar in nature to Aristotle's audience-oriented definition of tragedy in terms of the cathartic response it provokes.

A number of critics have attempted over the years to supply a version of the *Poetics* for comedy. Three of the better studies are Lane Cooper's *An Aristotelian Theory of Comedy,* James Feibleman's *In Praise of Comedy,* and Richard Janko's *Aristotle on Comedy.*[17] I am fully aware that there is a certain circuitous comic complexity in trying to apply a nonexistent definition, filtered through generations of critics, to a work of fiction, for which it would never have been intended had the definition ever existed. Just the certainty that Joyce would have loved the whole idea is reassurance enough of his comic affinity to make the effort worthwhile.

Let us begin with the most recent version of Aristotle's definition of comedy, as proposed by Janko: "A Comedy is a representation of an absurd, complete action, one that lacks magnitude, with embellished language, the several kinds of embellishment being found separately in the several parts of the play: directly represented by persons acting, and not by means of narration: through pleasure and laughter achieving the purgation of the like emotions. It has laughter, so to speak, for its mother."[18] Although we are not dealing with drama in *Ulysses,* the other aspects of Janko's definition seem to fit Joyce's novel perfectly. The basic absurdity of *Ulysses* lies in its representation of Bloom's life from the time he gets up on June sixteenth to the time he goes to bed on the early morning of the seventeenth as a complete action. Hugh Kenner has reminded us that even during that span of time much has happened of which we hear nothing.[19] This day in the life of a nondescript Dublin ad salesman, for whom nothing is resolved, especially when compared to Odysseus's adventures, makes a comic virtue of its lack of any magnitude in the Aristotelian sense.

No one would deny that *Ulysses* contains in every episode embellished language, which becomes more pronounced in the later chapters, where individual kinds of embellishment are peculiar to each episode. While Joyce's form of the comedy is fiction, its pleasure and laughter, for this reader at least, do bring about a form of purgation.

Cooper attempts to satisfy the question of what is purged by cathartic laughter by discussing a whole range of emotions, such as envy and anger, that might be substituted for pity and fear. However, the very subjectivity of Aristotle's definition of tragedy hinging upon audience reaction is compounded when we consider comedy, in which what is funny and what many define as comic may be different; even if we define comedy as what is basically funny, we open ourselves to a whole spectrum of debate. Henri Bergson's idea of funny business in his essay, "Laughter," for instance, strikes me as being a grim representation of the hapless, the infirm, and the mentally incompetent.[20] His depiction of man's malicious assault on mechanization through a humanized comedy is comparable to chuckling over the plight of AIDS victims. Yet even this strikes someone somewhere as funny: witness the recent spate of AIDS jokes. If there were no difference of opinion on the subject, there would hardly be a need for a study such as this.

One point on which most critics seem to be in agreement is Aristotle's broader view of the functions of comedy. Feibleman's assertion is typical: "Comedy ... concerns itself with ordinary persons, uses humble and everyday language, and resolves its complications in a fortunate ending."[21] Yet we will see that Joyce's language, as well as that of his immediate comic predecessors, is comedic in its irregularity, and his conclusion, like Sterne's, is ambiguous. Part of the divergence from an Aristotelian definition arises from the nondramatic genre, and part is because comedy is not a static, but a vital and evolving medium. In evolving from a lower, more primitive set of impulses, it is less stylized and traditional, less open to formal criticism, and freer by nature than tragedy to pursue its own shape and bent.

The result is a comic ambiguity that allows critics such as Feibleman to claim that the *Odyssey* is a great comedy, and still others, such as Wylie Sypher, to see comic elements in all of Kafka, *The Brothers Karamazov, Hamlet,* and even *King Lear.*[22] It also allowed Joyce to adapt an epic form for his novel and to transform the grimmest part of Odysseus's adventures, the revenge on the suitors, into the much more realistic comic equanimity of Bloom.

Comedy's refusal to treat pathetically the angst of human frailty confronting eternal verities is the most consistent factor in comic continuity. It moves critics like Elder Olson to see comedy as leading to valuelessness:

> Comedy ... removes concern by showing that it was absurd to think that there was ground for ... [painful emotion]. Tragedy endows with worth; comedy takes the worth away. Tragedy exhibits life as directed to important ends; comedy as either not directed to such ends, or unlikely to achieve them.
>
> If we call action of the latter sort *valueless,* we may define comedy as an imitation of a valueless action.[23]

Although, in fairness, Olson's quotation is taken out of context, his remarks represent a long tradition which comic writers have been warring against for more than twenty-five hundred years, as being contrary to reality. The liberating amorality of comedy in terms of its freedom from the tyranny of an established system of values provides its appeal to the audience. Somehow we always associate value systems with the *good,* even though such systems are often arbitrary and based on false premises. These myopic systems are the Quixotes of the world, going their way deprived of any Panzaesque antidote. Stephen's artistic follies in one respect are much better than the patriotic, rhetorical, religious, and bibulous foolishness of his fellow citizens: he has enough sense not to believe in them completely. On the other hand, Bloom is scarcely sure of anything ("Black conducts, reflects, [refracts is it?], the heat" [*U* 4:79 – 80; 1961:57]). He is slightly off base in his observations about nearly everything, from confused musical identifications, through the explanation of physical phenomena, to his interpretation of Roman Catholic ritual. Throughout, the long recitals of his stream-of-conscious uncertainties and errors provide a constant underlying comic pattern.

Joyce chose as his chief comic vehicle not a Falstaffian miles gloriosus, neurotically out to aggrandize himself, but a curiously self-possessed, generally deferential, ordinary man. I'm not sure that Bloom fits the Aristotelian comic bill as being greatly inferior to the audience. It is presumably because Bloom is so much like us that we identify much more with him than we would with our betters. Critics who see the novel as some sort of cosmic defeat for Bloom and, by extension, themselves as a part of the human race, effect an equal identification, while imposing their morosely existential view of life upon the novel. We yearn for answers to insoluble problems. If we don't get them in a novel any more than in our own lives, we say that the novel reflects the profound existential abyss of meaninglessness. Comedy, on the other hand, sees the irrelevance of those things which are horrors only if we regard them as such. Instead of Othello-like outrage at the violation of his marital bed, Bloom views it

> as natural as any and every natural act of a nature expressed or understood executed in natured nature by natural creatures in accordance with his, her and their natured natures, of dissimilar similarity. As not so calamitous as a cataclysmic annihilation of the planet in consequence of a collision with a dark sun. As less reprehensible than theft, highway robbery, cruelty to children and animals, obtaining money under false pretences, forgery, embezzlement, misappropriation of public money, betrayal of public trust, malingering, mayhem, corruption of minors, criminal libel, blackmail, contempt of court, arson, treason, felony, mutiny on the high seas, trespass, burglary, jailbreaking, practice of unnatural vice, desertion from armed forces in the field, perjury, poaching, usury, intelligence with the king's enemies, impersonation, criminal assault, manslaughter, wilful and premeditated murder. As not more abnormal than all other parallel processes of adaptation to altered conditions of existence, resulting in a reciprocal equilibrium between the bodily organism and its attendant circumstances, foods, beverages, acquired habits, indulged inclinations, significant disease. As more than inevitable, irreparable. (*U* 17:2178–94; 1961:733)

Bloom's reaction is certainly not Medea's, any more than *Ulysses* is a Greek tragedy.

In comic ignorance of the profundities which should be ruining or at least complicating his life, the comic protagonist concerns himself with such corporeal trivialities as flatulence,

constipation and its happy relief, elimination, and sex. Leopold
Bloom is just such a man, married to a like-minded woman.
That some critics see him as an Irish Willy Loman can best be
explained by the first reader-response critic, Aristotle, who, as
Cooper says, "advanced to the position that each distinct kind of
art must have a definite and characteristic activity or function,
and that this special function or determinant principle is equivalent to the effect that the form produces on a competent ob-
server; that is, form and function being as it were interchangeable terms, the organism *is* what it *does* to the person capable of
judging what it does or should do."[24] So, while many critics
laugh at *Ulysses*, they do not see it as a comic novel, because they
insist that it is more profound than comedy. Their misunder-
standing stems principally from the erroneous underlying assumption that comedy, despite its antique origins and its sem-
inal place in the beginnings of the novel, is somehow the inferior
because it is the more common genre.

There is a separate if not equally misled group of critics
who have taken the position that comedy, far from being value-
less, exists to point out the real foibles of mankind. They received impetus again from Aristotle, who said, "Comedy points
to what actually happens ... in the interests of what may happen."[25] This position led to the view that the value of Aristophanes' work lay principally in his satiric corrective of social
follies. While it is true that Attic comedy was founded on contemporary events and was harshly satiric of persons and institutions, this satiric potential should not lead to a definitive conclusion about the genre as a whole, any more than the comedy
of manners is representative of all aspects of comedy.

Joyce grew up in a country that produced many of the
greatest satirists of English literature, and no one will deny the
Irish gift for mimicry and ridicule. Obviously these forces are at
work in *Ulysses*, especially in the grand parodies of contempo-

rary and historical styles and events in the second half of the book. James Feibleman has based most of his work on comedy on the supposition that comedy, especially "good" comedy, is a principal didactic source of change. It is possible that Stephen's original idea in *Portrait* of forging the uncreated conscience of his race was pursued by Joyce through the comic medium of *Ulysses*. But if the harsher ironies of *Dubliners* didn't bring about any revaluations of national conscience, then the pleasanter ambiance of *Ulysses* would hardly have been the vehicle. Besides, Joyce believed enough in Stephen's theory that didactic or kinetic art is inferior not to sacrifice his own work on the altar of social instruction any more than did Swift or other great classic Irish satirists.

Like Aristophanes, Joyce got into trouble by making his contemporaries and their institutions sustain the brunt of his fictive gibes. The heirs of Reuben J. Dodd, I am told, are still in court. Fear of just such reaction contributed to Joyce's difficulties in finding an Irish publisher for his works. If Joyce occasionally mixed his humor with harsher satire, his main didactic thrust was toward the older, more profound lesson of comedy: that life, as difficult as it is, has a fluid continuity that can provide a sense of pleasure as well as pain, that in the seasonal cycle, following death there eventually comes a renewal, and that many of our difficulties are self-induced, and avoidable, if we only see their folly.

Having reaffirmed Feibleman's maxim that "comedy is an antidote to error,"[26] I sense a complacency in comedy, a presumption of the comic writer and his appreciative audience that they are able to share the *New Yorker* comic lens which restores proportion to a distorted and chaotic world. Sixty-five years after the publication of *Ulysses*, some of Ireland's problems have lessened, others have become more acute, still more remain constant, despite Synge, O'Casey, Joyce, a dozen contemporary comic writers, and Eamon De Valera. Perhaps comedy's lessons lie in acceptance rather than in change.

At any rate, the amorphous nature of comedy is generally agreed upon by most later critics. Sypher links the techniques of a number of tragedians and writers of more solemn fiction to comedy with the assertion (with which most of us would agree) that somewhere out in infinity comedy and tragedy merge. Hermione de Almeida stresses the seriocomic nature of life as Joyce and Byron see and reflect it in their style.[27] Perhaps, as Sypher says, life is so unpalatable that its grotesqueness produces a comic effect, especially in our "century of disorder and irrationalism."[28] That certainly would explain the presence of the black humor of books like *Catch 22;* however, the end Yossarian seeks is a pain-free existence in harmony with the natural order, the same as all of his comic predecessors.

The principal violating force of this natural existence is vanity. George Meredith agrees with Bergson that the remedy for vanity is laughter, but disagrees with Bergson's assertion that laughter is incompatible with emotion, and that once sympathy sets in, it is impossible to laugh.[29] Meredith's comedy would admit Dickens as high art, because Meredith's version of comedy is much closer to tragedy, but neither writer considers the fact that vanity is another name for hubris, which is a principal cause of tragedy. The point is that the pejorative connotations of *vanity* seem to conflict in many Western minds with the dignity of exalted stupidity in the form of hubris. The latter is aggrandized by dint of its being associated with the nobler tragic impulse, while its counterpart, vanity, is devalued because of its commonness among ordinary people. It is just such elevated preconceived notions that the satiric aspects of comedy seek to debunk. Thus, Joyce's shift to comedy was almost inevitable. He had a satiric mind which was sensitive to the ludicrous to begin with. A comic mentality is too realistic to embrace for long the exalted idea of becoming a Moses for one's race. Joyce's ordinary, comic Messiah was a more likely candidate, with his creator, like God, somewhere behind the scenes paring his fingernails.

The amorphous nature of comedy, because of its realistic treatment of all human activity and thought, creates a spectrum of applications in our attempts to fix categorical definitions upon it. When Frye observes, "Comedy ranges from the most savage irony to the most dreamy wish-fullfilment romance," he really has not gone far enough.[30]

In *Partial Magic* Robert Alter examines the reflexive novel genre by singling out for extended treatment books that I would define as comic novels.[31] It is gratifying to see *Ulysses* among Alter's choices. The basis of the connection lies in the amorphous nature of the comic genre which admits nearly everything into its province. The incongruity of authorial intrusions is a case in point, as is their destruction of illusion through constant reminders that the work itself is an artificial construct.

The question of comedy's place in art is fundamental to our consideration of the Joyce canon, especially because art provides the fulcrum of interest in *Portrait* and is carried by Stephen into the opening of *Ulysses*. The earlier novel never loses its concern with the topic of artistic creation, from its title to its narrative perspective, which is shaped by the consciousness of its artistic protagonist. Art constitutes the subject of lengthy discussion in the last chapter, and the question of the relation of Stephen to the creator of *Portrait* lingers throughout. The novel is a working illustration of the relationship between the artist and his creation on the one hand, and life on the other. At the beginning of *Ulysses,* through the medium of stream-of-consciousness, we move objectively into the mind of the artist, Stephen, and, beginning with Calypso, into the mind and life of his worldly counterpart, Bloom. The novel broadens its sphere of interest to become a one-day snapshot of a city. Bergson defines such a situation as comic: "Comedy lies midway between art and life. It is not disinterested as genuine art is. By organising laughter, comedy accepts social life as a natural environment; it even obeys an impulse of social life. And in this respect it turns its back upon art, which is a breaking away from society and a return to pure nature."[32] If Stephen's artistic perceptions play a major role in the first three episodes, their comic counterparts dominate the rest of *Ulysses*. In calling attention to the artificiality of the artistic creation, the self-reflexive novelist would certainly disagree that art returns "to pure nature" rather than being at best a good imitation. Joyce poses the question comically by translating it into terms of a dispute between high art and comedy: between Stephen's view that art is a pure embodiment of epiphanic truth, and Bloom's view that art can be turned into a guinea per column, and, even more pragmatically, into an absorbent piece of toilet paper.

To serve the practical ends of comedy there are at least two typical comic profaners in *Ulysses*, Bloom and Buck Mulligan. Wylie Sypher describes the character type: "The sacrifice may be interrupted by an unwelcome intruder (an *alazon*) who views the secret rites; he is a profaner of the mysteries, an alien. This character must be put to flight or else confounded in a 'struggle' that may also occur in the form of a catechism, to which he does not know the proper answers. In either case there is a debate, a dialectic contest."[33] Bloom makes profane Stephen's divine mission of art, just as he silently denigrates the religious rites in All Hallows and the cemetery chapel. We will see in the chapter on comic narrative that the egregious violations of aesthetic sensibility in the Bloomian style of Eumaeus are a projected literary endeavor of Bloom's, after his completion of a lucrative column or two for *Titbits*. The catechetical debate Sypher refers to takes place, of course, in Ithaca, where many of the answers, in the form of Bloom's opinions and memories, when not false or misleading, are certainly confused.

It is even easier to see Mulligan's role as profaner. While Buck may be perfectly at home ridiculing church ritual and doctrine, he is equally adept at poking malicious fun at Stephen's artistic pretences ("He proves by algebra that Hamlet's grandson is Shakespeare's grandfather and that he himself is the ghost of his own father" [*U* 1:555 – 57; 1961:18]. Their early morning repartee is nothing so much as Mulligan's attempt to arouse a reluctant Stephen to debate the merits of his theories of artistic creation and their relationship to the priest's role in the transubstantiation process.

If comedy sports its traditional profaners, they are only a part of the admittedly low nature of the comic enterprise. Cooper tells us that Aristotle recognized the nature of comedy's origins, discussed earlier: "The *Poetics* frankly recognizes the origin of comedy in the phallic procession and dance, without the least indication of censure."[34] As we have seen, the great antiquity of comedy accounts for the obscene features of old comedy carried down to modern times as frank physicality in the novel. As Sypher says, comedy finds the lowest or most primal common denominator of human response.[35] Our recognition of such shared and often repressed facts of life in a comic situation induces the pleasure of laughter, which is in Aristotelian terms the source of catharsis.

Joyce's propensity to combine the gross with the sublime thus approaches comedy in two ways: first, in his erudite and elegant literary analogies and in his parody of literary pretensions, Joyce pursues the high comic road, linked to the satiric corrective to human vanity; and second, in his depiction of the pleasures and pains provided by the functions of the human body, Joyce admits his comic vision to the oldest and, if not the most dignified, certainly the most timeless aspects of human nature. The end is pleasure. Cooper tells us, "If the catharsis involved in laughter has something to do with the reproductive and excretory functions, with our thoughts about them, or with the subconscious or unconscious aspects of them, then the element of 'pleasure,' to which beauties of structure, of persons, of diction and metre, of melody and 'spectacle,' contribute, plays its part in this catharsis."[36]

Violations of tradition in the cause of commonsense reality are the hallmarks of comedy. If comedy sets out to destroy human pretension, certainly a fair target is an author's propensity to regard his art as akin to Stephen's divine epiphany. Reduced to mundane comic terms, art is an exercise in craft, possibility, and illusion, with its authority, as we have learned from Aristotle, stemming from its audience's reaction. Comedic art, whose principal end is to provide pleasure, realistically works toward this end in the ultimate satisfaction of its protagonist; tragedy satisfies the audience, not the protagonist, who encounters towering dilemmas that the normal audience can recognize only as metaphors of their most exalted fears and aspirations. Members of an audience composed of normal (nonacademic) readers are not likely to kill their children or husbands, commit incest with their mothers, or be called upon to avenge their fathers' murders; yet they can derive a certain pleasure from representations of the events of their own lives: the change of seasons, a good bowel movement, masturbatory relief, or a pork kidney, for instance. Other human activities are of a nature we have come to consider more seriously—cuckoldry, the search for identity, and threats to family security—and it is in imitating actions such as these that comedy approaches tragedy and runs the risk of enlisting our sympathy.

Lest we get too maudlin in our pity and fear, comedy also provides distance through the mechanisms of ludicrousness, and pretension, and so forth, and through their attending language and characterization. If in the process such traits as vanity are held up to chastizing ridicule, then that is an additional benefit which might promote healthy change. Satiric works that exist solely for that purpose, however, are as far removed from the central comic impulse as are sermon tracts. Neither *Animal Farm* nor *1984*, for example, is funny; yet their bizarre premises hover on the fringes of comedy, as do most activities in which humans sporadically engage. If it happens, or could happen, some comic writer will eventually deal with it. Witness the recent spate of comic horror movies, such as *An American Werewolf in London*. Comedy has the effect of domesticating the wildest fears as well as fancies of man. To turn horror into pleasure by a low form of familiarization rather than an exalted identification with aspiration is the unique attribute of comedy.

Viewed in a solemn light, Bloom's situation has all the makings of pathos, not joy. He is an outcast from the society of his fellow Dubliners, cuckolded and abused, and a failure at his livelihood, almost certain never to foster the progeny or the political, social, or economic future he fantasizes. During the course of his day, his one bid for a change in life, his invitation to Stephen, is rejected, and his wife's final idyllic vision of him is murkily blended with an earlier memory of bringing Mulvey off into her handkerchief.

Yet few of us exhibit a great deal of sympathy for Bloom, because he is a competent as well as keyless citizen; gifted with a comic native intelligence; able to take abuse without caving in, even, when need be, amply defending himself; humane and sensitive to others rather than selfishly preoccupied with the wrongs done him; and basically accepting of the lot life has to offer. Essentially, Bloom is a pretty healthy character in a novel that becomes increasingly comic in its narrative incongruities and in its recapitulations of basic themes.

Plot was for Aristotle the major component in the composition of tragedy, and much of the *Poetics* revolves around such ancillary factors as recognition and reversal. Both episodic and unified plots may occur in comedy, of course, and one is hard put to judge whether in as free and undefined a genre as comedy one type is better than another. However, in Aristotle's name

Cooper categorically condemns episodic comic plot as the worst type.[37] Far be it from Cooper to admit the *Odyssey* as great comedy. The idea of *Ulysses* as a comic work muddies the structural waters still further. Since Joyce didn't specify divisions as *chapters* per se in the final manuscript for his novel, critics, not wanting to be redundant, often use the terms *chapter* and *episode* interchangeably. *Episode* seems to fit the epic Joyce admittedly was parodying, but *chapter* seems more in keeping with the intricately woven fabric of *Ulysses*. A linear time sequence distinguishes the relative position of events, which, unlike many of those in the *Odyssey*, are inextricably interdependent upon each other. While the episodes occur at different places and, after the early morning, at successive hours, after the manner of many picaresque adventures, their mutual dependence upon each other for meaning is as often achronological as not. The importance of Boylan's visit, for instance, is not immediately apparent in Calypso, and Bloom's early thoughts about Boylan are not fully understandable or justified until four o'clock. The throwaway newspaper in Lotus Eaters seems unimportant, but the rhubarb in Cyclops comes as a direct result of Lyons's misinterpretation of Bloom's remark in the earlier meeting. This incremental doubling effect of events as well as characters is nowhere more apparent than in Circe, where the surreal scenes recapitulate earlier events and ideas. If, as Cooper says, comedy's "essence is the imitation of things seen out of proportion," Circe is the most comical of all the chapters, and its laughter more cathartic than frightening.[38]

In Aristotelian terms, I read *Ulysses* as containing a minor reversal of fortunes (at least in the readers' minds) from bad to good, or, to be more precise by being less precise, from ambiguous to confidently ambiguous. Neither Bloom's nor Stephen's lot changes much, but I'm not sure their fortunes are so bad at the beginning. Neither do their conditions substantially decline nor are they overpowered, even during Circe, when Bloom and

Stephen are most vulnerable. I think I join the average reader in the certainty that by the end of *Ulysses* Bloom at least has the wherewithal to cope with his problems.

Feibleman and others have seen contemporaneity as an essential feature of comedy:

> Sherwood Anderson is speaking for all comedians when he exclaims, "I want to take a bite out of the now." Comedy epitomizes the height of the times, the *zeitgeist*. Hanging upon the vivid immediacy of actuality, it touches the unique particularly embodied in the passing forms of the moment. A criticism of the contradictions involved in actuality, it must inevitably be concerned with the most ephemeral of actuals. Since its standpoint is always the logical order, it deals critically with the fashions of specific places—because they are not ubiquitous, and with those of specific times—because they are not eternal.[39]

No one will deny the immediacy of the Dublin scene on June 16, 1904, as depicted in *Ulysses*. No novel has ever been so firmly rooted in the time, place, and events of its day, nor has any concerned itself so much with those events we normally think of as ephemeral. *Ulysses* itself has engraved them so deeply on the stone of immortality that Joyceans still go to buy their lemon soap bars at Flynn's and attempt to pay Bloom's library fine. Such events occur regularly at Dublin Joyce Symposia, where Joyce's comic spirit reigns. The designation *Bloomsday* is itself a token of homage to the importance of comic trivia.

By way of recapitulation, I would like to conclude this chapter with a condensation of Cooper's eleven-point summary of where Aristotle stands on the effect of comedy.[40] Its application to *Ulysses* is mostly obvious, but I cannot resist the temptation of occasionally editorializing. My comments on Cooper's points appear serially in italics.

1) Unlike tragedy, the characteristic of comedy is not the arousal of pity and fear.

Critics who see "Ulysses" as ultimately tragic must have made some sort of piteous or fearful identifications.

2) The proper effect of comedy is some form of pleasure.

3) The pleasure should be aroused in the right sort of spectator, a mature person of sound reason and correct sentiment; not necessarily an expert, but a person of taste and culture.

If most Joyceans, who are obviously persons of taste and culture, could remember their initial reading of "Ulysses," I am sure that they would think first of the comic pleasure they derived before the book became encrusted with erudite interpretation.

4) The imitation is a realistic portrayal of the common events of human life rather than of the extraordinary ones of tragedy.

5) The pleasure derived is associated with the perception of a defect or ugliness that is neither painful nor injurious.

This may be the sticking point for many Joyceans who see any realistic depiction of life as automatically painful, or injurious, or as representing the special angst of meaninglessness.

6) It is a pleasure similar to the one produced by the *Odyssey*, without the disastrous consequences to the suitors. Enemies walk off the stage as friends, without any one slaying or being slain.

Even if Bloom could never be Blazes's buddy, still Bloom rejects his bloodiest thoughts in Ithaca. Joyce's comic deflation of the revenge patterns Bloom considers is the basis of one of the funniest passages in the novel:

What retribution, if any?

Assassination, never, as two wrongs did not make one right. Duel by combat, no. Divorce, not now. Exposure by mechanical artifice (automatic bed) or individual testimony (concealed

ocular witnesses), not yet. Suit for damages by legal influence
or simulation of assault with evidence of injuries sustained
(selfinflicted), not impossibly. Hushmoney by moral influence,
possibly. If any, positively, connivance, introduction of emulation (material, a prosperous rival agency of publicity:
moral, a successful rival agent of intimacy), depreciation,
alienation, humiliation, separation protecting the one sepa-
rated from the other, protecting the separator from both. (*U*
17:2200–2209; 1961:733–34)

7) The pleasure produced by comedy on the audience or
reader is "psycho-physiological," outwardly demonstrated by
laughter.

8 and 9) Among accessory means to the effect of comedy
are music and the marvelous.

*The first is present throughout "Ulysses," especially in the form of
the musical comedy of Sirens, and the second permeates the longest
chapter in the book, Circe.*

10) Recognitions and reversals afford pleasure in comedy
as well as in tragedy. While normally the reversals of comedy are
from worse to better, if the opposite occurs it will not be serious
or painful.

*Even if there is a painful reversal for Bloom in his recognition of
Molly's infidelity, his masochism comically turns it into pleasure.*

11) As tragedy produces incidents of *pathos* or suffering,
comedy contains an incident or incidents of a ludicrous or especially hilarious or joyful sort.

*The examples from "Ulysses" that I have interpolated into this
book are just the tip of the comic iceberg.*

Throughout the research on this chapter, though admittedly undertaken to fit *Ulysses* into prevailing comic theory, I was
hard-pressed to find any variation on the theory that would not
admit Joyce's novel. If Joyce is well within the theoretical framework of comedy, he is also, as we shall presently see, in the great
tradition of comic novelists.

Comic Narration

๙**D**uring the last part of the seventies and the beginning of the next decade, the Joyce industry turned its most astute observers loose on the problems of the narrative patterns in *Ulysses*. Two books especially, Marilyn French's *The Book as World* and Karen Lawrence's *The Odyssey of Style in "Ulysses,"* were landmark studies offering new insights into structure and meaning through close scrutiny of Joyce's narrative techniques.[1] Other critics, such as Robert Adams and Michael Groden, have divided the novel into two or three segments based not on plot or characters' acquisition of the knowledge traditionally gained in the novel form, but on shifts in the narrative pattern from the "initial style" to a variety of narrative experiments in the later chapters.[2] Joyce is said to have lost interest in writing in his "initial style," which itself includes a variety of narrative innovations, such as portmanteau words, a shifting of perspective to accommodate the focal character of the sequence, and stream of consciousness. He moved in the latter half of the book to a variety of parodies or imitations of styles found in the daily press, in pulp publications, in classical English literature, and in the speech of his contemporaries in turn-of-the-century Dublin.

What most critics who have studied the narrative techniques have failed to discuss at any length, perhaps because it is so obvious, is that the change in narrative pattern also signals a change from serious, or at least realistic, to comic intent. The language becomes increasingly parodic. While funny things can be expressed in everyday language, as they are in the early chapters of *Ulysses,* that sort of comedy is associated with humor rather than wit. I define humor in the traditional sense, as the product of normal occurrences and foibles that we instinctively recognize as the universal, even if perhaps a bit bizarre, incongruities of human life. Wit, on the other hand, is the product of intellect, of language rather than action, of linguistic incongruities. As such, parody, satire, and its first cousin, the burlesque of style, are the intellectual equivalents of the humorous activities and speech of ordinary people. The universal application of parody to all things and people links it to the comic, carnival genre Mikhail Bakhtin has so brilliantly delineated:

> To the pure genres (epic, tragedy) parody is organically alien; to the carnivalized genres it is, on the contrary, organically inherent. In antiquity, parody was inseparably linked to a carnival sense of the world. Parodying is the creation of a *decrowning double;* it is that same "world turned inside out." For this reason parody is ambivalent. Antiquity parodied essentially everything: the satyr drama, for example, was originally the parodic and laughing aspect of the tragic trilogy that preceded it. Parody here was not, of course, a naked rejection of the parodied object. Everything has its parody, that is, its laughing aspect, for everything is reborn and renewed through death.[3]

When Joyce's novel became lopsidedly parodic, it made an unmistakable declaration of comic intent.

In the later episodes of *Ulysses* the speech of institutionalized characters such as the barfly and the citizen exist alongside the styles of depersonalized institutions such as the catechism, scientific methodology, and the popular women's magazine. In the earlier chapters such characters as the anglophilic Mr. Deasy represent character prototypes. However, their language is not the center of the narrative focus, but merely spoken or quoted material within the overarching narrative framework. The point is that as the focus shifts to more linguistic variation, the tone of the book becomes more playful and less seriously tragic or painful.

Readers, generally frustrated by the difficulties of comprehending the pyrotechnics of narrative shifts and by having to negotiate a new agreement with regard to narrative expectation with every successive episode, attempt to make sense out of the apparently frivolous, and search ever more intently for answers to the narrative riddle, at the same time they are searching for ultimate answers to the book. If critics fail to find the answers, they are apt to call the lack of ultimates a profoundly existential answer in itself. But nowhere in the later episodes of *Ulysses* can I find any form of narrative parody or distortion that produces a serious or tragic reaction rather than a comic one. Comic storytellers, from Chanticleer's erudition to Lucky Jim's paper on "Merrie England," have traditionally attempted parodic narration. Add to that the Irish penchant for mimicry and you have the portmanteau styles of the later *Ulysses*.

The narration of the Telemachea is controlled by Stephen Dedalus. As we have seen, his are the fictions, the motifs, the correspondences to which we devote ourselves in order to make traditional sense of the rest of the action of the novel. We look for father-son parallels, artist as subject-creator, guilt, and oedipal themes because Stephen has pointed us in those directions. But his is a literary, pattern-seeking mind full of himself and of history. Of such narrative stuff is Oxen of the Sun made, only to degenerate into nearly unintelligible babble. The narration of the initial Bloom chapters reflects his status as allroundman, a servant of the press, an advertising salesman who moves among typesetters and political institutions in a world consisting of popular periodicals and clichés. It is traditional to say that he represents a scientific outlook and Stephen a catechismal one. I'd like to take the observation a step further, and declare that all of the narrative patterns of the later episodes are projections essentially of the two protagonists' individual and collective imaginations and experiences.

I wish to deal in this chapter with the comic aspects of a fiction-making literary mind which could transform windmills into giants, or, in Oxen of the Sun, a bee sting into the wound of a dragon's spear, and an open can of sardines into "a vat of silver that was moved by craft to open in the which lay strange fishes withouten heads" (*U* 14:149–51; 1961:387). If Stephen's actions are not inherently funny, then the literary and ecclesiastical sources of his projections, when used to describe realistic daily existence, can be. The joint sensibilities ultimately compose *Ulysses*. A Bloomian mentality gives us the humor of the novel, and a Dedalean one the wit.

I would like to return to a previous point: that the "initial style" provides not only the narrative norm, which is constantly returned to in the latter half of the book, but also the fundamentals of the plot, allowing the reader with some difficulty to piece together a reasonably coherent action despite the narrative distortions inhibiting our easy understanding. All novels contain a covenant of narrative convention between reader and author, a covenant that determines how the novel is to be related and what will or will not be within the parameters of acceptability. For instance, fantasy and science fiction circumscribe their own realms within the first paragraphs. So too does the style of most genres announce certain conventions and limitations upon itself, such as the credibility of the narrator. We do not expect violations of these norms, though often they are violated by authorial intrusion and the like. To proceed through six chapters before encountering more than minor shifts in narrative tone, then to have the intruding headlines in Aeolus announce a change before subsequently returning to the initial style for three more episodes, is likely to produce in the reader of the last eight episodes a feeling of betrayal of the narrative covenant.

Sirens is really the pivotal chapter in the narrative transformation. Though it contains the verbal innovations of the overture and an abundance of musically allied sounds, Sirens remains fundamentally within the initial style, and although Bloom's mind has already established a prevailing humor for the book, the comedy—that is, wit as well as humor—is not predominant until Cyclops. The only genuinely sustained comic wit in the first eleven episodes is the introduction of the headlines in Aeolus. The chapter foreshadows not only later narrative changes, but also a change from a serious to a comic mode.

The narrative variations after Sirens produce increasingly funny reactions right through the comic masterpiece of Ithaca. As the reader's frustration level mounts, so do the comic distortions of reality, until the very covenant itself becomes a prime source of comedy. I had never realized just how funny Ithaca was until I heard a substantial portion of it read aloud at Franklin and Marshall College during a Joyce celebration. It took an actor with a highly developed sense of verbal incongruity to turn tedium to hilarity. Likewise, an older, practiced ear with a penchant for the antique is more likely to appreciate the comic exaggeration of cliché piled on cliché in Eumaeus, simply because of the scope of the exaggeration. Long out of currency, many of the expressions sound more like tired phrases. That is probably why so many Joyceans until fairly recently dismissed the style of the episode as "tired," rather than regarding the style as spectacular verbal play.

To demonstrate that the narrative perspectives of the latter chapters are consistent with one of the greatest comic novels in 380 years, I will discuss a few examples from Aeolus before outlining the comic narrative devices of the second half of *Ulysses*.

AEOLUS

The headlines' break with traditional narration in Aeolus simultaneously introduces a new comic effect. The distancing that results from the late addition of the headlines follows the traditional pattern of comic wit by purposely divorcing the reader from pity and fear, from being caught up in the action. Like the characters in Aeolus, the narrator, fascinated by his own rhetoric, disregards the human drama of Bloom's rejection in the editorial room.

The putative subject of the editorial room conversation, rhetoric and style divorced from meaning, provides the key to comically meaningful depiction of meaninglessness in the last half of *Ulysses*. The characters are talking about rhetoric for its own sake. They praise Taylor's speech, given in rebuttal to Fitzgibbon's earlier rhetorical trumpeting, not for what he said but for the language in which he said it. So the ten commandments, certainly a meaningful group of injunctions to many in Western civilization, become less important than the language in which they are couched. The examples the Aeolus characters offer are extended anecdotes designed to prove the rhetorical virtuosity of the speakers themselves. Each one seeks to outdo the rhetorical flourishes of the previous speaker, just as Taylor linguistically bested Fitzgibbon's speech on the same subject, language, that night at the College Historical Society. In Aeolus the Phoenix Park murders assume less importance than the way in which Gallaher reported them, the story of the Taylor-Fitzgibbon debate tops that, and, finally, building on Taylor's theme of the Promised Land, Stephen returns the entourage to Dublin and the Messianic motif with which the chapter began. But his rendition of a degraded Dublin and the Pisgah sight of two old mid-wives is designed less to provide a truthful vision than to impress its hearers with Stephen's clever rhetoric.

The whole business is not very funny until the headlines are added. Like the rhetoricians of Crawford's office, the nar-rator of the headlines seeks distance from the realities of the sit-uation being reported. The headlines, like the modes of rhetoric in the popular press which they emulate, are the products of self-aggrandizement, beginning with the overly formal and pro-ceeding through a staccato barrage to a largely unsuccessful ex-ercise in satiric wit. What is funny about the headlines is not the intentional satire of their descriptions, but the pretenses of the headline-writer. The narrator of the headlines is just as deluded as everyone else, and in his effort to be increasingly impressive and funny, he becomes the butt of his own joke, even as he seeks to degrade Stephen's attempts at rhetorical self-aggrandize-ment. For example, the last headline,

> DIMINISHED DIGITS PROVE TOO TITILLATING
> FOR FRISKY FRUMPS. ANNE WIMBLES, FLO
> WANGLES—YET CAN YOU BLAME THEM?
> (*U* 7:1069–71; 1961:150)

is almost as long as the text it introduces. The chapter depicts a collection of rhetorical Quixotes, including Stephen and the nar-rator of the headlines. In Aeolus Joyce announces an all-out comic war on the pretensions of narrative method.

SIRENS

In Sirens, the transitional chapter, the tone if not the shape of the narrative changes more radically and consistently than in previous chapters. The emphasis shifts to sound rather than meaning. Like music, the chapter is built around the production, physics, articulation, phonetics, and interpretation of sound. The announcement of a new narrative departure in the overture, which links sounds rather than meanings, is also an announcement that *Ulysses* will explore radically different narrative techniques. Musical, prosodic, and artistic preoccupations will be redefined for the novel genre, previously regarded as the literary form most resembling normal discourse. Onomatopoeic devices abound in closer, more literal imitation of the nonlinguistic sounds of life: clocks, cash registers, boots scraping the floor, harness bells, door knockers, nose snufflings, all noises announcing only themselves, and not linguistic signals of abstract meaning.

Music is the closest artistic parody of purely natural or manufactured sound without meaning. But songwriters were soon joined by lyricists who domesticated musical sounds with words, as more and more contrivance and artificiality were built into the form to impose meaning upon it. What was once an experiment in emotion-producing mathematical vibrations became inundated with manufactured meaning. Songs became operas, and operas musical comedies as conceit was heaped upon conceit, until the art form became a parody of the lyrics which themselves parodied life.

In an earlier book, I concentrated for the most part on the meaning of the lyrics in the 158 references to forty-seven songs in the episode. But the concept of lyrics itself constitutes a form of sirens' song, because lyrics are a linguistic distortion of an abstract art, music, to invest it with literal meaning. Joyce added still another auditory dimension to the Sirens narrative, a series of verbalized nonverbal sounds, such as the tuning-fork call: "From the saloon a call came, long in dying. ... A call again. That he now poised that it now throbbed. You hear? It throbbed, pure, purer, softly and softlier, its buzzing prongs. Longer in dying call" (*U* 11:313–16; 1961:264); or Simon's playing the piano trill between the lines of "Goodbye, Sweetheart, Goodbye": "A duodene of birdnotes chirruped bright treble answer under sensitive hands" (*U* 11:323–24; 1961:264); or the oft-quoted sound of Simon's high B flat at the end of *M'appari:* "It soared, a bird, it held its flight, a swift pure cry, soar silver orb it leaped serene, speeding, sustained, to come, don't spin it out too long long breath he breath long life, soaring high, high resplendent, aflame, crowned, high in the effulgence symbolistic, high, of the etherial bosom, high, of the high vast irradiation everywhere all soaring all around about the all, the endlessness-nessness......" (*U* 11:745–50; 1961:275–76).

Joyce's descriptions are as close to representing musical tonality as any writer is likely to come. Its excess is comic but its effect, comic truth. The purely auditory functions of the episode are further underscored by a focus on two characters, the blind piano tuner and Pat the deaf waiter, who manage to exist quite well because of or in spite of their adaptation to their auditory surroundings. Pat is oblivious to most of the noise and the singing, but the piano tuner not only hears better than anyone else, as Bloom observes, but also is ultimately responsible for the one pure musical sound in the episode by leaving behind his perfect-pitch tuning fork. Thematically the piano tuner's imperfection, cursing, links him to the croppy boy who "cursed three times since last Easter Day," and hence to Stephen, who, like croppy, failed to pray for his mother's rest. All thematic motifs in *Ulysses* are suspect, slightly off center, and of course there is little reason to associate the piano tuner with Stephen, except for Joyce's numerous hints of a possible musical connection through the motif. Certainly Bloom's helping the piano tuner cross the street parallels later events in the novel, but that is a far cry from the speculations to which Joyce has led us with his linguistic clues linking the tuner and Stephen with the innocent and maligned croppy boy. The perfect pitch emanating from the tuning fork is both a siren's song and an assertion that its message and motif are true. In Sirens sound seems to be truth and meaning is suspect.

The comic aspects of the Sirens' narrative style draw upon all of the above musical and sound devices, though it is not until the end of the episode that the variations on the narrative achieve a fully comic resolution rather than being merely pleasing or aesthetically appeasing. The conclusion of Sirens announces a new comic strategy in which four of the six remaining chapters will conclude on comic notes, leaving the reader amused rather than merely reflective. In Sirens, as in these later chapters, the comic narrative conclusion draws parodic meaning from motifs developed during the episode.

The songs of the Sirens episode have largely been about love in the first half and war and patriotism in the latter part. The two themes coalesce in Robert Emmet's patriotic and sacrificial love for his country and the love of Christ for man in his sacrifice on Calvary, both of which are juxtaposed against the random sounds of chinking glasses, lurching trams, and Bloom's flatulence:

> Bloom viewed a gallant pictured hero in Lionel Marks's window. Robert Emmet's last words. Seven last words. Of Meyerbeer that is.
> — True men like you men.
> — Ay, ay, Ben.
> — Will lift your glass with us.
> They lifted.
> Tschink. Tschunk.
> Tip. An unseeing stripling stood in the door. He saw not bronze. He saw not gold. Nor Ben nor Bob nor Tom nor Si nor George nor tanks nor Richie nor Pat. Hee hee hee hee. He did not see.
> Seabloom, greaseabloom viewed last words. Softly.
> *When my country takes her place among.*
> Prrprr.

Must be the bur.
Fff! Oo. Rrpr.
Nations of the earth. No-one behind. She's passed. *Then
and not till then.* Tram kran, kran, kran. Good oppor. Coming.
Krandlkrankran. I'm sure it's the burgund. Yes. One, two. *Let
my epitaph be.* Kraaaaaa. *Written. I have.*
Pprrpffrrppffff.
Done. (*U* 11:1274–94; 1961:290–91)

In a juxtaposition of hearing and sight, Bloom sees Emmet's picture in the window and reads the hero's last words. When Bloom introduces Mercadante's oratorio in comparing Christ's last words with Emmet's, he adds a musical dimension to the setting. In doing so, he confuses Meyerbeer, a Jewish composer not especially enthralled by the crucifixion, with Mercadante. In any case music is incongruous to either scene. The idea of Christ warbling the words from the cross is rescued from ludicrousness only if the last words are perceived as the convention of a great work of religious art, and Mercandante's oratorio is not generally regarded as such. It is closer to Monty Python's musical version of Christ's last words, "Always look on the bright side of life," which draws upon the incongruity of a musical crucifixion for its comic effect.

In the conclusion, Sirens' lyrics metamorphose into speech as the song "The Memory of the Dead" is seized upon by the drinkers as a meaningful way to put their patriotism to use as an excuse for another sip of booze. The sound of the clinking glasses, meaningless in itself, is followed by the tiptapping of the entering blind man's cane. The piano tuner, whose hearing, like Pat's sight, has to do double duty, is deprived of Bloom's ability to view the last words of Emmet, just as Pat earlier was deprived of the ability to be moved by the sound of the music from the bar. It is unclear whether when Bloom says "softly," he means softly reading the last words aloud, or attempting to fart softly under cover of the passing tram, or whether he is devising some other combination of inspirational language and random noise. Whatever measure of control Bloom has over the volume of his fart, however, it is by no means certain that he is gifted enough to produce such generally accidental occurrences on cue to accompany memorable last utterances.

The fart is probably a happy comic coincidence, sound given meaning through juxtaposition with high sentence, as Joyce mocks excessive and often hypocritical interpretation with the randomness of noise made meaningful. With the word *Done* we see an end to the language of sentimental patriotism and religion and we begin in earnest a new comic attitude for the book and a new flippant source of virtuosity in literature.

CYCLOPS

In Cyclops Joyce takes both the high and low roads, contrasting the meanness of vision and speech of the barfly with the turgidity of an all-enumerating omniscient narrator who piles list upon list, example upon example, so that excess of expression is matched by the excesses of enumeration. Clearly the duet of narrow-minded, drink-cadging pettiness and overabundant fulsomeness is an apt portrayal of the barroom historians who wax so eloquent in Barney Kiernan's. Mean and unflattering personal histories are mixed with nationalistic diatribes reflecting the spectrum of prejudices, both by the barfly and by his drinking cronies. The comedy stems from the contrast between the dual narrative voices, each parodic in its own way. The barfly's observations are a collection of clichés, his descriptions the hackneyed metaphors of contemporary Dublin pub life. There are so many that their use, excessive as it is, takes on its own comic exuberance. The other voice, as a number of critics have pointed out, is an ever-shifting montage of ceremonial excesses of figures of speech and verbal pretensions which rapidly abandon verisimilitude for linguistic ostentation. If the barfly's sneering descriptions are an intentional parody on that unworthy drinker's part, then the high tone of the hyperomniscient narrator is aggrandizement carried to its extreme. Critics such as Geoffrey Hartman have found fault here with the self-consciously derivative nature of Joyce's parody.[4] But, as we will see with Rabelais, Cervantes, and Sterne, excess is the key to comedy. Hartman's remarks might be appropriate to high, serious fiction, but they are the very source of the debunking quality unique to comedy.

The excesses of Joyce's parody infuse the chapter with a genuine comic energy which is only hinted at in earlier episodes. French is correct in observing that the omniscient narration with all its aggrandizements neutralizes the meanness of the characters and the episode generally.[5] The narrators purposely fail to enhance the importance of the action, and instead tend to diminish it comically through comparison to the excesses of Ireland's sentimentalized view of itself. For the reader jaded with historical rhetoric, it offers paradoxically a comically revitalized sense of the injustices done to Ireland even while the advocates of Ireland's grandeur are being made to appear inherently foolish.

There is little need here to reiterate the varieties of parody that have been systematically catalogued by others, or to reiterate that most critics have realized how funny the chapter is. It is enough to say that Joyce, like the comic playwrights of the Dionysian festivals, violated the boundaries of literary decorum with the same exuberance as he rejected the high sentence of tragedy. The result was the sneering corrective of comic reality, again not far removed from Rabelais, Cervantes, and Sterne. Karen Lawrence points out that the degenerative quality of the hyperbolic lists of guests and ceremonies "is reminiscent of what happens when Don Quixote attempts to use the language of romance."[6]

Joyce again concludes the episode with a comic climactic paragraph blending the two narrative voices and undercutting any more solemn vision of Bloom espousing his doctrine of love to the crucifying rabble:

> When, lo, there came about them all a great brightness and they beheld the chariot wherein He stood ascend to heaven. And they beheld Him in the chariot, clothed upon in the glory of the brightness, having raiment as of the sun, fair as the moon and terrible that for awe they durst not look upon Him. And there came a voice out of heaven, calling: *Elijah! Elijah!* And he answered with a main cry: *Abba! Adonai!* And they beheld Him even Him, ben Bloom Elijah, amid clouds of angels ascend to the glory of the brightness at an angle of for-tyfive degrees over Donohoe's in Little Green street like a shot off a shovel. (*U* 12:1910–18; 1961:345)

The passage is a pastiche of the description of Christ's transfiguration (Matthew 17:1 – 5) and Elijah's appearance on the mountain. At least one of the words ben Bloom Elijah cries, "*Abba*," is ascribed to Jesus in Gethsemane, and the capitalization of the masculine third person pronoun is a convention usually reserved for Christ or God. But according to Dowie's throwaway it is Elijah who is coming, and Elijah also makes a glorious ascension into the firmament. Thus Bloom becomes a combination prophet resembling the dual narrators of the chapter who have spelled out the evils and delusions of contemporary Dublin.

The last prepositional phrases of the paragraph, beginning "at an angle," signal a return to the voice of the barfly, whose limited vision of heaven is circumscribed by Donohoe and Smyth, Grocers, Tea, Wine and Spirit Merchants. The last phrase brings us back to earth at the same time that it reinforces the incongruity which is the basis of comedy.

NAUSICAA

Nausicaa again uses the device of contrasting narrators, the first a return to Joyce's *Dubliners* habit of suiting the narration to the mind-set of the character described. Like the narration of both barfly and omniscient narrator in the previous episode, the technique in Gerty's half of Nausicaa requires a corrective on the reader's part to extrapolate a more accurate view of the action from the report of an obviously flawed narrator, whose women's magazine perspective has obviously dominated Gerty's thinking. Distortion here takes on a subtle turn, as Gerty uses the perspective to mask the truth of her own infirmities, and to provide a romantic rationalization for her mundane existence. Since pitiable character foibles provide most of the humor, the comic aspect of the stylistic parody seems much more muted than in the previous episode. Statements such as "Gerty was dressed simply but with the instinctive taste of a votary of Dame Fashion" (*U* 13:148 – 49; 1961:350) are easy enough to rectify in the reader's mind, and we can move easily between the fantasy of the literary influence and the meanness of her unaffected thought: "Gerty wished to goodness they would take their squalling baby home out of that and not get on her nerves, no hour to be out, and the little brats of twins" (*U* 13:404–6; 1961:357). Her weakness matches the size of her distortions, which need no comic elaboration, and so wit becomes secondary to bathos. The worship of the Virgin associated with the Star of the Sea church provides only a light comic background for Gerty's romantic distortions.

The counterbalancing palliative is Bloom's stream of consciousness in the latter half of the chapter. Gerty's fantasies provide her relief from her mental distress, but Bloom's masturbation, with all its climactic fantasies of Molly and Blazes and all its voyeuristic fetishism, is an eminently practical solution to the problem of his arousal. As Bloom takes matters in hand, so too does the narration as it coincidentally switches from Gerty's fantasy to Bloom's practical perversion. The fulcrum in the shift from Gerty-dominated narration to a Bloom-dominated narrator is also the crux of Gerty's insecurity:

> She walked with a certain quiet dignity characteristic of her but with care and very slowly because — because Gerty MacDowell was...
>> Tight boots? No. She's lame! O!
>> Mr Bloom watched her as she limped away.
>>> (*U* 13:769–72; 1961:367)

Thus we instantly learn something that answers a number of problems regarding Gerty's feeling about her companions throughout the entire first half of the chapter, something that the narration, because of its approximation to Gerty's mind, has withheld or distorted beyond recognition. This is not the case with the narration that accompanies Bloom's direct stream-of-conscious thought. During the rest of Nausicaa little narration intervenes between Bloom's mind and the reader. Any distortions of reality are not stylistic but purely cerebral on Bloom's part. What few third-person narrator lines there are introduce new stream-of-consciousness paragraphs with a description of Bloom's activity ("Mr Bloom with careful hand recomposed his wet shirt" [*U* 13:851; 1961:370]). These represent an objective factual return to the initial narrative style, the first of many times that the initial perspective will be reclaimed throughout the rest of the novel.

Only in the brief concluding paragraph do we return to Gerty's narrator:

> because it was a little canarybird that came out of its little house to tell the time that Gerty MacDowell noticed the time she was there because she was as quick as anything about a

thing like that, was Gerty MacDowell, and she noticed at once
that that foreign gentleman that was sitting on the rocks looking was

> *Cuckoo*
> *Cuckoo*
> *Cuckoo.*
>
> (*U* 13:1299–1306; 1961:382)

The sound of the cuckoo blends the two perspectives into a possible statement about Bloom's mental condition, though critics
have often seen it as a statement about his marital condition. If
the sound is produced through Gerty's distorted narrative, then
the craziness or cuckoldry implied may itself be suspect. Nothing, after all, in Gerty's previous thoughts has indicated Bloom
to be a cuckold, or even a little dotty. The time is nine o'clock.
The last three *cuckoos* complete the knell previously reported by
the initial style narrator, so it is reasonable to assume that Gerty's speculation was broken off before we knew what her conclusion was. The situation at the end of the chapter mirrors that of
the middle, when we fail to learn whatever she was going to conclude about herself in the transitional sentence that ended her
segment of the episode. All of this is, of course, linked to
Bloom's inconclusive statement etched in the sand. The uncer-
tain conclusion will become standard throughout the later episodes. The comedy of the conclusion of Nausicaa, like the end of
Sirens, stems from the incongruity of combining random noise
with supposedly meaningful speculation.

OXEN OF THE SUN

Karen Lawrence offers the following pronouncement on
the comedy of language in Oxen: "One can find comic incongruity in 'Oxen' (the sardine tin is an example), but in general
the emphatic exuberance and spontaneity of the early chapters

are rare in 'Oxen,' which seems more craftsmanlike in its execution."[7] Other critics, such as Eliot, see Joyce as exposing "the futility of all English styles."[8] Indeed, most of the utility is produced by the reader's having to make repeated correctives to the distortions of successive narrators in order to ascertain the action taking place. Although the sources of the embryonic narratives are "literary" for the most part, and the quality of Joyce's mimetic accuracy has been attested to by numerous scholars, the linguistic genius of the parody and its prototypes obfuscates and distorts the action, leading to the conclusion that the more genius the writer exhibits, the more he biases the work. The reader is called upon to negotiate a new compensatory agreement with every shift of narrative parody, enabling the dragons' spears to be translated into bees' stingers, and so forth.

The assumption of all of this parody is essentially comic: that literature, even in its attempt at fictive verisimilitude, has nothing to do with reality, but exists as a fictional conceit, shaped by the writer ultimately to glorify its own perceptions. Writers of serious or somber fiction, no matter how distorted their vision of reality may be, do not seek the sort of list-making aggrandizements that undermine their own purpose. Accuracy dictated that Joyce's mimicry of serious styles in Oxen not violate the internal integrity of the parody with comic extravagances of the sort common to Cyclops. The humor of the episode is predominantly ironic, the product of our consciousness of the magnitude of distortion writers build into their narratives.

The speeches of the characters, who burlesque themselves as well as their literary prototypes, make most of the comedy of the episode, at least until the end, when, after the birth of the word, the embryonic specimens of literary artifact become the fully developed word-infants of contemporary dialect. After the utterance of the word, there is a brief literary multistylistic chorus before the coda of multifarious dialects, beginning "All off for a buster." That the next five pages contain even greater distortions than the rest of the chapter is evidenced by the numbers of continuing panels and discussions which they inspire at Joyce symposia.

But ultimately comic relief from the purgatory of narrative confusion is at hand with Dowie's salvational message:

> Come on you winefizzling, ginsizzling, booseguzzling existences! Come on, you dog-gone, bullnecked, beetlebrowed, hogjowled, peanutbrained, weaseleyed fourflushers, false alarms and excess baggage! Come on, you triple extract of infamy! Alexander J Christ Dowie, that's my name, that's yanked to glory most half this planet from Frisco beach to Vladivostok. The Deity aint no nickle dime bumshow. I put it to you that He's on the square and a corking fine business proposition. He's the grandest thing yet and don't you forget it. Shout salvation in King Jesus. You'll need to rise precious early, you sinner there, if you want to diddle the Almighty God. Pflaaaap! Not half. He's got a coughmixture with a punch in it for you, my friend, in his back pocket. Just you try it on. (*U* 14:1580–91; 1961:428)

Dowie's speech really doesn't afford much in terms of improving the readers' spiritual well-being, but it does indeed provide a cough mixture for linguistic inflammation, a concluding burst of understandable comic exuberance to reinforce the episode's murky comic prognostication that little meaning can ever come from either literature or language in general.

CIRCE

Circe is undeniably a funny episode. The projection of Bloom's aspirations for political and religious leadership, his fears and trials, his fetishism and masochism are all comically objectified during the chapter; however, there is little comedy inherent in the language of the narration. The incongruity lies in the scenes described, such as the construction of the new Bloomusalem, *"a colossal edifice with crystal roof, built in the shape of a huge pork kidney, containing forty thousand rooms."* (*U* 15:1548– 49; 1961:484)

The language of the characters is often comic and exaggerated, but the only narrative voice in Circe consists of stage directions, which, although they may describe fantastic events and scenes, are delivered for the most part in neutral terms, unaffected by variations of parody or aggrandizement. Since the stylistic variations from complete objectivity are so few, it might be worth while to comment on the three most obvious: *"Time's livid final flame leaps and, in the following darkness, ruin of all space, shattered glass and toppling masonry"* (*U* 15:4244–45; 1961:583). This quotation, lifted from Nestor, trivializes Stephen's idea of the significance of his breaking Bella's chandelier by loading the description with his earlier Blakean apocalyptic imagery. Here, at the climactic moment, the stage directions and the mind of a protagonist seem to coalesce. The result is ironic more than comic.

The second variation of the normally bland narrative style of the stage directions appears to have a more comic effect: *"They blow ickylickysticky yumyum kisses"* (*U* 15:4321; 1961:586). Here the narrator may have merely chosen the most accurate and economical, albeit extralexical, adjectives to describe the whores' solicitations.

The final example is made genuinely comic by adding a musical distortion to the description: *"The car jingles tooraloom round the corner of the tooraloom lane. Corny Kelleher again reassuralooms with his hand. Bloom with his hand assuralooms Corny Kelleher that he is reassuraloomtay. The tinkling hoofs and jingling harness grow fainter with their tooralooloo looloo lay"* (*U* 15:4916–20; 1961:608). It is simply not in Joyce's plan to be perfectly consistent in any narrative agreement. There has to be at least one violation.

There is much verbal comedy in Circe, but the comedy of Circe stems primarily from the incongruity of the concocted visions, the memorably affected comic speeches of Dowie and Mulligan and the rest as projections of Bloom's insecurities, rationalizations, and ambitions, funny because they depict the low comic Sancho Panza attitude with which we can readily identify. But the resulting comedy and parody are not produced by the narrative method of the episode, and are addressed elsewhere.

EUMAEUS

The confrontation with the unconscious in Circe is the structural climax of *Ulysses*. Despite its humor, the episode arouses an unease akin to the pity and fear of tragedy. In Eumaeus, Joyce allows us to recover from the shocks of the Walpurgisnacht with soothing Bloomian comic platitudes and clichés. Fitzharris's shelter, for all its sinister characters and overtones, has a comfortable lack of clarity about specifics and an overlay of clichés and lies which plaster the open psychic wounds of the objectified subconscious. Language obscures, like a layer of oily bilge the sailor spreads on the troubled waters of meaning. The comforting message of the three turds, to be read like tarot cards on the floor, is that significance and horse manure are indistinguishable. Yet we persist in extracting meaning from the seeming convergence of completely disparate minds as they make their way to Eccles Street talking of "sirens, enemies of man's reason, mingled with a number of other topics of the same category, usurpers, historical cases of the kind" (*U* 16:1889 – 91; 1961:665), to the tune of "The Lowbacked Car," which seems to point to some form of nonexistent unity, but which refers merely to the cabman's vehicle.

The chapter is a brilliant exercise in comic obfuscation. It represents the mundane circumlocutions of the sort Bloom would have offered had he indeed written *My Experiences in a Cabman's Shelter*. The episode is as much a stylistic projection of

Bloom's mentality as Oxen of the Sun was of Stephen's, and it has a comic vitality ignored by early critics whose mentalities resemble Stephen's more than Bloom's. The episode provides an encyclopedia of linguistic atrocities. Mixed metaphors, forced puns, excessive pretensions to elegance such as coyness and cuteness, and fastidious identification of pronoun antecedents are overlaid with commonplaces, forced idioms, and tired sayings. But a Nabokovian appreciation of linguistic pop art emerges from the excess of schlock, a comic celebration of the enormity of the violation of sensibility such narrative provides, until ironically we recognize the pretenses of our own violated standards. The narration of Eumaeus has the same comic acceptance of the world as Warhol's can of tomato soup.

The comic aspect of the narrative pretensions is intensified, as it was in Cyclops, by its proximity to an even lower form of literary ineptitude. The funniest sections of Eumaeus are those involving the description and dialogue of D. B. Murphy:

> —Chews coca all day, the communicative tarpaulin added. Stomachs like breadgraters. Cuts off their diddies when they can't bear no more children. See them sitting there stark ballocknaked eating a dead horse's liver raw.
>
> His postcard proved a centre of attraction for Messrs the greenhorns for several minutes if not more.
>
> —Know how to keep them off? he inquired generally.
>
> Nobody volunteering a statement, he winked, saying:
>
> —Glass. That boggles 'em. Glass. (*U* 16:479–486; 1961:626)

Murphy's faith in the power of his own untutored word rivals the narrator's own pretensions. Like *Burke's* in Oxen or *plastics* in the film *The Graduate*, the word *glass* takes on its own inane immortality, at the same time that it gives an additional dimension to linguistic pretention.

Lawrence and French both assert that Bloom's mind as reflected in his earlier stream-of-conscious thought passages is incapable of producing anything as egregiously bad as the narration of Eumaeus.[9] Neither seems to understand that were Bloom to attempt to produce a literary artifact, he might well employ the linguistic atrocities everywhere present in Eumaeus. Composition teachers frequently encounter opinionated, slightly inferior students, whose language becomes transformed by the literary aspect of their task into exactly the same sort of cliché-riddled pretentiousness as the narrator's in Eumaeus. Bloom had neither the skills nor the background to avoid it. At any rate, Joyce would have enjoyed the prospect of critics disagreeing over whether a fictional character would or would not have had the appropriate skills or lack of them to write a chapter Bloom never had an opportunity to write in the first place. Of such stuff is comedy made, to modify an old adage.

ITHACA

Ithaca comically anticipates our near desperation for answers to the traditional questions of fictive meaning, for relationships between characters and events, and for patterns that will establish some significant artistic intent in order to justify the reader's epic struggle for understanding. We are by this time as much the objects of our own pity and fear as are Stephen and Bloom. Despite Aristotle's notion that the purpose of poetry is to provide pleasure, we are still entranced by our hope for meaningful lessons. Sure that there are truths to be gained from *Ulysses,* we believe that if they have thus far eluded us it somehow is our fault, and the epiphany will come in the concluding pages.

Here in Ithaca the narrator asks the questions and answers them in cold prose, which if it is not clear, then at least it is matter of fact. There are answers to questions we would never ask, as well as to ones we want desperately to know about. The relationship between Ithaca's questions and answers is disconcerting, however. To questions demanding speculative interpretation, we get answers of fact, and vice versa, and so many relationships abound that their irrelevancy to what we want to know makes them appear like an infinity of microcosmic and macrocosmic meaningless possibilities, even though Joyce has only begun to explore the potential. Once relevancy is divorced from our expectation of meaningful literary patterns of truth, the possibilities are endless, as are the possibilities of the comic sensibility which insists that things, events, and people can simply exist without necessarily being aspects of any moral pattern. The essence of tragedy lies in our fitting the characters' actions and circumstances into significant truths about human nature and in the didactic certitude that life, with all its comic accidents and irrelevancy to moral patterns, harbors some deeper, underlying significance. If there is any didacticism in comedy, it is that the tragic view itself is unrealistic.

What makes Ithaca so funny is the purposeful confusion of relevancy and irrelevancy: of human nature and the empirical world we live in ratified by the recital of facts that seem randomly relevant and irrelevant, and the whole framed in a catechetical system of questions and answers originally designed to prove with rhetorical certainty the existence of the unknowable. The incongruity of such an assortment, coupled with a plethora of unrelenting details, provides a modern Shandyism which is every bit as funny as it was two hundred years ago. Joyce's reflexive questioning of the process of the novel itself, begun here, entirely pervades his last and admittedly more comic work, *Finnegans Wake.*

If the narration of Oxen obfuscates our understanding of the events by imposing skewed literary interpretations upon their representation, then Ithaca obscures interpretation by providing us with a welter of undifferentiated facts. If literary meaning breeds chaos, so too does empirical observation.

Joyce's parody of the literary and empirical points of view affords us a distancing comic lens which corrects the distortions of any sentiment and profundity we might try to impose on the novel.

The universal truths of serious literature are essentially presented in microcosmographic form. Oedipus's search for the truth about himself, Odysseus's homecoming, and Aeneas's political abandonment of Dido all give us insights about our own individual lives, but those insights are at least partially self-aggrandizing aspirations for significance in a world of random, mundane, and irrelevant detail. Comedy, Ithaca itself, if anything, tells us that the mundane and trivial are all right, that they are the stuff that human experience is really all about, and that insignificance is not shameful.

The comic aspect of irrelevancy is most obvious in Ithaca when Joyce plays with the irrelevancy of language itself. In the series of questions about the differences and similarities between Bloom and Stephen we find the following:

> Did he find four separating forces between his temporary guest and him?
>
> Name, age, race, creed.
>
> What anagrams had he made on his name in youth?
>
> Leopold Bloom
> Ellpodbomool
> Molldopeloob
> Bollopedoom
> Old Ollebo, M.P. (*U* 17:402−9; 1961:678)

The silliness of the anagrams foreshadows the narrator's later creations of *Stoom* and *Blephen,* in which critics (myself included) have seen much transformative significance. The anagrammatic answer in the above quotation responds to an irrelevant follow-up question to a potentially meaningful answer. The sequence is comic, and the result, in realistic terms, is inane. The anagrams sound like something meaningless which Bloom or any child might make, and the resulting names sound as comical as they are devoid of meaning.

The theme of verbal meaninglessness is picked up again several pages later in a discussion of Plumtree's Potted Meat, when we are admonished about false labeling: "The name on the label is Plumtree. A plumtree is a meatpot, registered trade mark. Beware of imitations. Peatmot. Trumplee. Moutpat. Plamtroo" (*U* 17:603–5; 1961:684). Could there actually be four spurious imitators hoping to capitalize on the integrity of the Plumtree label? More likely the comedy is both an exercise in verbal irrelevancy and an admonition not to be fooled by the game any more than by the label.

The episode builds again to a comic crescendo in the description of Bloom's reactions to his cuckoldry, and then diminuendos with an enumeration of Bloom's company in his *Arabian Nights* travels: "With? Sinbad the Sailor, and Tinbad the Tailor and Jinbad the Jailer and Whinbad the Whaler and Ninbad the Nailer and ... [etc.]" (*U* 17:2321–23; 1961:737). Contrary to Lawrence's idea that the names on the list following Sinbad's are merely nonsensical variants produced by the semiconscious mind of Bloom as he drops off to sleep, at least Tinbad, Jinbad, and Whinbad were actually characters in the long-running sequels to the Christmas pantomime.[10] Popular themes were repeated yearly, and the 1892 edition of Sinbad proved so popular that it was revived again and again, sometimes under Sinbad's name, and once under the name of Turko, a popular character in the Sinbad production. The formula remained constant, but the songs, skits, and jokes varied from year to year. Versions of the *Arabian Nights* are still current in contemporary pantomimes. What appears to be nonsense is not always irrelevant any more than facts always have meaning.[11]

Thus, a chapter that we had hoped would lead us to meaning gives us facts — sometimes false facts — but stubbornly refuses to yield up easy meaning. Since irrelevancy and frustration are hallmarks of comedy, Joyce's circumlocutions in Ithaca inspire a sort of comic abandonment if we only relax and enjoy ourselves.

PENELOPE

The concluding episode returns to a largely unpunctuated variation of the initial style, and to humor from the wit of linguistic fireworks and incongruity. It is funny in its own incongruous sentimentality, suggesting that there is a dominant order to events. But if Molly's eternal affirmation seems apparent, it is also the opening line to the chorus of a comic music-hall song, "Yes because he never did a thing like that before" (U 18:1; 1961:738),[12] and we are on thin critical ice if we apotheosize Molly's observations as the ultimate answers to the modern dilemma, the universe, or whatever questions we think the novel raised. The last soliloquy is a celebration, and the final comic language is that of the critics who interpret a series of concluding affirmatives as negatives or extrapolate a positive or negative universe on the basis of whether Molly will cook breakfast in the morning. More problematical than even the culinary dilemma is whether any ultimate conclusions about life's meaning or patterns can ever be confidently extracted from *Ulysses*. For the moment, at least, I am much happier with the view that *Ulysses* is a magnificent comic celebration of life.

Comic Predecessors

⁊⁊This chapter will investigate three comic predecessors of *Ulysses,* not in an effort to establish that Joyce somehow used the plots, characters, or themes of great comic writers before him, but in order to show that he participated in a long-standing comic tradition, which occasionally produces, consciously or not, remarkable similarities between *Ulysses* on one hand and *The Heroic Deeds of Gargantua and Pantagruel, Don Quixote,* and *Tristram Shandy* on the other. Whether these specific earlier works established a comic narrative methodology or whether the narratives give evidence of an archetypal tradition is not at issue here. Obviously a number of other writers such as Fielding and Byron have worked in the tradition. Hermoine de Almeida, to whom this chapter is indebted for a number of insights, traced the comic tradition from Homer to Joyce (by way of Byron).[1] The reasons for choosing the three works I did from among all of Joyce's comic predecessors are that *Don Quixote* and *Gargantua and Pantagruel* have only recently been considered at any length in this light, and that Joyce critics have rightfully regarded Sterne's contributions to *Finnegans Wake* as paramount, and as a result have had concomitantly less to say about *Tristram Shandy* and *Ulysses.* Ultimately, what underlies this chapter is the hope that the comparisons can make a contribution to our recognition that *Ulysses* is principally a comic novel, which emulates its comic predecessors much more closely than critics have hitherto recognized.

RABELAIS

Scholars have long sensed Joyce's affinities to Rabelais, but only in the last ten years has the subject been dealt with at length. Joanne Rea's dissertation, "Rabelais and Joyce: A Study in Verbal Humor," concentrated on *Finnegans Wake,* while John Kidd's dissertation, "Joyce's Debt to Rabelais," focused on *Ulysses.*[2] Kidd's work anticipated some aspects of the following discussions on catalogues, cuckoldry, and giganticism. Oddly, Joyce denied reading Rabelais before writing *Ulysses,*[3] though a direct reference to Rabelais's account of Gargantua's birth appears in Molly's soliloquy.[4] Aside from this, there is a silence on Joyce's part regarding the indebtedness of *Ulysses* to Rabelais, though he was flattered by Larbaud's and Jaloux's comparisons of *Ulysses* with Rabelais's works.[5]

When Albert Jay Nock and C. R. Wilson said of Rabelais, "his work is an extraordinary mosaic, a miscellany of nearly everything known or knowable in his time," they might have taken comfort in the fact that their subject (like Bacon, about whom others made the same claim), lived most of his days in the sixteenth century.[6] But even for that age such speculation sounds hyperbolic. The point is that Rabelais, despite his considerable achievements in other fields, is principally recognized today as a comic writer, and the tradition of erudition, of literary precedent, is at least as important or perhaps even more important in comedy than in serious or tragic works. If, as we have seen, comedy often chooses the mundane or low aspects of human behavior as its subject, its satiric roots run deep, and erudition is the fertile soil on which it is nurtured, from Aristophanes to John Barth. It is worth restating that comedy thrives on common sense and the foibles of human activities seen through the mirror of past precedents both comic and serious, while most often tragedy is the product of passions and the flaws in human nature which imply an overarching, unquestioned natural law or morality.

Historical erudition juxtaposed against common or even crude activities supplies the incongruity out of which comic wit is born. The Renaissance origins of the novel at last afforded a larger canvas for a cosmic comic picture, which the serialized tales of Boccaccio and Chaucer could only begin to paint. Rabelais bridged the gap between short stories and the novel, between Odysseus and Tom Jones, between Dante and Milton, and between Greco-Roman classics and Cervantes. Rabelais's five books of the adventures of Gargantua and Pantagruel are epic road adventures given a ribald comic twist, an underground parody of Dante's divine vision, with Rabelais's ultimate word in a wine bottle — a biblical parody of the life, lessons, and pronouncements of physically larger-than-life embodiments of human perfection in the form of a hedonistic, all-wise, and nonjudgmental father-son team who seek to learn rather than to rule. Like Quixote and Stephen, they apply first to books for answers and to associations with fellow-learners, but after taking all that formal education can offer, they set out to discover the realities of everyday life.

The precursor of Cervantes, Sterne, and Joyce in developing literary allusion as a prime comic form, Rabelais, with his extravagant imagination, pushed the topic of erudition beyond the limits of hyperbole to include a scholar, Thaumast, whose thoughts and arguments were so profound as to be incapable of being rendered in words, and who debated the topics with Panurge entirely in the gestures of a dumbshow. Like Joyce in Bloom's Hades trip to Glasnevin, Rabelais includes an infernal visit in the tales of his overgrown Odysseuses and their companions. Epistemon's death and resurrection result in an account of hell in which Dante's discussions with the damned are parodied with a comic enumeration of the hellish occupations of the famous deceased figures of literature and antiquity. There is a typically Rabelaisean blatancy in the author's announcement of his intent to go to the ends of the classical world for Pantagruel's adventures.

In emulation of Dante's three female intercessors, Pantagruel's three queen-priestesses cure the infirm with songs and exist to fulfill their own whims and to keep the sacred fountain of water which can be transformed by imagination into wine. Of course, at the end of the long journey, Pantagruel's vision of ultimate truth takes the form of a bottle.

Besides the *Odyssey* and *The Divine Comedy* as prime sources of parody, Rabelais, like Joyce, frequently chose the Bible, from Gargantua's miraculous birth out of his mother's ear, through the sixty "begats" tracing the history of Gargantua and Pantagruel's lineage, to their parallel learning experiences in the first two books, which closely resemble the stories of Christ's youthful confounding of learned mentors. By the time Rabelais finished his five volumes, his aim was less didacticism than entertainment. Although he professes to have no moral purpose in the early books, the solemn wisdom of the mature Gargantua often seems like piety thinly disguised, and the Utopian vision of Gargantua's Thelemite Abbey, where all live in complete freedom, has overtones of moral instruction. That was to fade away in the later books.

Whatever lessons Stephen might have learned in a more conventional novel were to fall by the comic wayside as Joyce also changed intentions in the midstream Aeolus episode. Joyce's comic vision was to be ultimately closer to creating a "dramatic" work that would more successfully distance the author from his work than would a more solemn novel. When Rabelais was accused of creating blasphemous, heretical, antifeminist, anti-scholastic, obscene literature, his answer was always that he was trying to create a harmless entertainment. And he did manage, in that unmanageable work, to remain remarkably objective and detached from the comic views of his characters of whatever persuasion, while at the same time portraying the pretenses of most of the public and private activities of the Renaissance world.

His attacks upon the law are given in several forms, including the gobbledygook of legal terminology, when Pantagruel hears an indecipherable case and renders an opinion in similar terminology which satisfies everyone; the prevalence of perjury, when people go to school so that they can testify to anything; and the arbitrary nature of judgments, when Bridlegoose, an exemplary judge, admits that his decisions were based on rolls of the dice. Rabelais's continual satire on ecclesiastical practices and orders is a trait that Joyce, of course, shared, along with a satiric view of such social propositions as the virtues of economic prudence, and the objectives, risks, humiliations, and lusts of the marital state. In these, among scores of other tangentially treated topics, Rabelais and Joyce represented a panorama of the contemporary life of their day.

The institution of marriage provided the basis for much of the fiction of both Rabelais and Joyce. Panurge's decision regarding whether to marry provides the framework in which three of Rabelais's five books are set, with Book 3 exploring in hyperbolic detail the wisdom of an undertaking sure to culminate in Panurge's cuckoldry, and the remaining books dealing with voyages in search for definitive answers to Panurge's marital problem. From the instruction of the Shakespeare motif in the first episode, *Ulysses* is similarly preoccupied with the marital dilemma and cuckoldry. The problem assumes major importance with our introduction to the Bloom household and reaches a crescendo in the concluding pages of Molly's soliloquy. Her opinions regarding cuckoldry and Bloom's success as a modern-day hero are frequently seen by critics as ultimate answers to the book. Although marital fidelity has been a major factor in tragedy (witness *Hamlet* and *Othello*), it is perhaps even more common in comic plots, such as fabliaux, chiefly because it is so much a part of human life in all ranks and castes. In Rabelais, the problem is considered and discussed principally by a bachelor, with appeals to experts, some who have been married more than once and some not at all. However, Gargantua's wife, Badebec, the only wife and mother in the work, figures only in her widower's grief at her death in giving birth to Pantagruel. In the construction of the utopian Abbey of Theleme, little or nothing is made of the marital state, since it plays little part in a completely free existence.

Joyce was, of course, infinitely more careful in composing *Ulysses* than was Rabelais in writing his narrative, in which his lack of consistency is oft cited by critics and scholars. For example, from story to story the giants, Gargantua and Pantagruel, vary in size, from normal-sized men to beings large enough to cover entire armies with their tongues. Other inconsistencies abound in plot, character, and event, making Rabelais's volumes crude by comparison with Joyce's tight novel. The plot repetitions of Books 1 and 2 and the reverse order of their first appearance are a part of a pioneering venture conceived as a romp, disclaiming high seriousness. Rabelais tells us often enough in his introductions to the separate books that he doesn't give a fig for any criticism that presupposes a serious intent.

Joyce, on the other hand, makes no such disclaimers. Had he done so there would be no need for a book such as the present study to make the case for Joyce as a comic writer. First, as we have seen, there was the shift in Joyce's narrative methodology after the first few chapters, resulting in an increasingly comic persuasion in *Ulysses*. Further, I would argue that in confounding normal expectations, Joyce went beyond mere innovation to shift the emphasis of the novel from serious to comic. Yet we still try to treat it as if it were principally a somber novel, even realizing the impossibility of assuming such a stance with its successor, *Finnegans Wake*. In Joyce's writing, the thin lines between irony and satire and between satire and burlesque were crossed long before he began to compose the *Wake*. One result of the increasing blurring of these distinctions is the tightness of design in *Ulysses* and the apparent Rabelaisean looseness of the *Wake*. *Ulysses* seems to offer both a tight design and the abandonment of forms, at the same time that the book strives to be the epitome of exactitude in the modern novel.

This is not to say that traditional elements of comedy are not present in the early pages of *Ulysses*. If Joyce and Swift were accused of cloacal obsessions, Rabelais would seem to have been wholly preoccupied with elimination, both as metaphor and as process. Bloom's little endemic of a tablet of cascara sagrada hardly compares to the scene in Book 2 of *Gargantua and Pantagruel,* where men are encapsulated in gondolas and dispatched to Gargantua's bowels to shovel out the obstructions in his constipated digestive tract. Neither Stephen's nor Bloom's piddly piddles, even when jointly micturated, can compare with the drowning deaths of entire invading armies in Rabelais's classic giganticized urinations.

Elimination in all its forms, from Gargantua's farting grotesque little men to Bloom's flatulent comments on patriotism and religion, has always been a low if perennial source of comedy, because comedy exploits the familiar or earthy. The differentiation between the higher and lower bodily poles was recognized long before Bakhtin, but his application of the concept to comic regeneration is memorable:

> "Downward" is earth, "upward" is heaven. Earth is an element that devours, swallows up (the grave, the womb) and at the same time an element of birth, of renascence (the maternal breasts). Such is the meaning of "upward" and "down-

ward" in their cosmic aspect, while in their purely bodily aspect, which is not clearly distinct from the cosmic, the upper part is the face or the head and the lower part is the genital organs, the belly, and the buttocks. These absolute topographical connotations are used by grotesque realism, including medieval parody. Degradation here means coming down to earth, the contact with earth as an element that swallows up and gives birth at the same time. To degrade is to bury, to sow, and to kill simultaneously, in order to bring forth something more and better. To degrade also means to concern oneself with the lower stratum of the body, the life of the belly and reproductive organs; it therefore relates to acts of defecation and copulation, conception, pregnancy, and birth. Degradation digs a bodily grave for a new birth; it has not only a destructive, negative aspect, but also a regenerating one. To degrade an object does not imply merely hurling it into the void of nonexistence, into absolute destruction, but to hurl it down to the reproductive lower stratum, the zone in which conception and a new birth take place. Grotesque realism knows no lower level; it is the fruitful earth and the womb. It is always conceiving.[7]

In a sense comedy gives the lower bodily functions the regenerative equivalent of a divine natural purpose, and their exploitation in the comic works of Rabelais and Joyce is not only justified, but sorely needed to restore, regenerate, and correct the sterility of unnatural societal attitudes.[8]

Bloom's comic vitality embraces not only his appreciation of the basic bodily functions, but his recognition of their interdependence with the cycle of life and death. His speculations in the Hades episode on graveyard copulation and the pleasant sentience that rats enjoy in Glasnevin continue a series of comic life-in-death images beginning with the sperm-stained seats in the funeral carriage and Dodd's son's resurrection. The priest's traditional eternal-life prayers are interrupted by Bloom's stream-of-conscious insistence upon the distended quality of the priest's belly as Bloom consistently moves from north to south bodily poles.

At the other end of the honorific spectrum, both Rabelais and Joyce make their home towns the "holy" cities of an idealized existence. Chinon, Rabelais's birthplace, is engraved with the triumphs of Bacchus, while the new Bloomusalem is created in the shape of a huge pork kidney.

The methodology of Circe was almost inevitable if Joyce were to attempt to include Rabelaisean excesses in a modern novel. What better vehicle than to trace their logical origins in a Freudian unconscious? The scheme provided Joyce with a virtually boundless vehicle for Rabelaisean comic grotesquerie played off against the realistic scene in Bella's brothal. Joyce could blend modern realism with comic surrealism at the same time that he presents us with some of the most hilarious scenes in twentieth-century literature.

Joyce followed Rabelais's pattern of comic excess in other ways and in other chapters also. Rabelais was a master at digression, which was easier in the days when the novel was still in its embryonic stage and the final shape of its evolution from the short story or tale was not yet completely developed. James Feibleman was the first critic to recognize this tendency in Joyce's work: "The rippling flow of the vast catalogues, which show Rabelais alive to everything, remind one of nothing so much as of the contemporary *Work in Progress* by James Joyce."[9] As is the case with many other techniques developed in the *Wake,* Joyce performed his initial experiments in *Ulysses.*

In Rabelais whole chapters abound on subjects completely extraneous to the plot, and by Book 4 of *Gargantua and Pantagruel* Rabelais had adopted a journey-tales structure by which he was even less constrained by the necessity of keeping a continuous narrative thread running through his material. Joyce's departures from the story line, even in the last half of *Ulysses,* are of course less frequent than they are in *Wake*, and there is always a greater danger in *Ulysses* that what appears to be a mere digression might provide some key element in the plot.

But Joyce recognized that digressions were a staple of comedy, especially those that took the form of exaggerations, like the detailed list of books in Bloom's library, resembling the 140 titles Rabelais enumerates in the St. Victor's Library. While these lists, grown comic by their gigantic proportion, appear in nearly every chapter of Rabelais's works, their use in *Ulysses* is confined to the later episodes of the book. Joyce's lists have about them a parodic quality, such as the giganticizing narrator's descriptions of events, processions, and the like in Cyclops.

Despite the digressions, Rabelais's present Book 1 is closer to the form of the modern novel than his later books would promise to be. After he succeeds in ridding his father's kingdom of the invading army and establishing a utopian Abbey, Gargantua's activities, which had begun in Saturnalian license, end in the platitudes of wise governance. The likelihood of his son Pantagruel's following in the same staid steps for three additional books was mitigated by a trickster figure, Panurge, who constantly operated on the fringes of the law and decorum, to provide a new source of Bacchanalian comedy. That Panurge, who initially possessed all the right morally reprehensible traits, such as cowardliness and self-aggrandizement, is later intermittently depicted as brave and selfless is the product of Rabelais's inconsistency rather than of design. At any rate, like Buck Mulligan, Panurge has a strong sense of the incongruous, and attempts to outrage decorum for its own sake. His friendship with the wise Pantagruel is reminiscent of Falstaff's relation to Hal, and, like Shakespeare in writing *The Merry Wives*, Rabelais didn't know when to stop. As his comic figure inevitably became beloved both by the populace and Rabelais, Panurge assumed almost a commanding role in terms of the plot. The voyages were taken at his behest, and he had as many adventures as his master in the later books.

Perhaps profiting from Shakespeare's lessons, Joyce never let Mulligan dominate the scene for long. After Telemachus, Mulligan appears for any length only in Scylla and Oxen, though Joyce couldn't resist giving him a brief but hilarious disquisition on Bloom's sexual tendencies in Circe. Following Cervantes's lead, as we shall see, Joyce used his trickster figure for comic relief, while at the same time affording his character a sinister as well as comic aura.

Rabelais opened the door of comedy to extended fiction. By his exuberant irreverence for the staid institutions of the church, the courts, and social decorum, by stressing the laughable realities of a peasant life shorn of platitudes, and by comically exaggerating the pretences of his society, Rabelais provided a model for future comic novelists, from Cervantes, Fielding, and Sterne, to Joyce, Barth, Amis, and Nabokov.

CERVANTES

Joyce critics have long known—indeed Joyce has admitted publicly in *Finnegans Wake*—his use of, if not his adulation of, Laurence Sterne.[10] Cervantes was another matter. No reference to him appears in any of Joyce's published letters, and Ellmann records only one remark regarding Joyce's estimate of the earlier writer, a passing reference to the superiority of the *Odyssey* to *Don Quixote* and other great works of Western literature.[11]

Cervantes himself had something in common with both Stephen and Bloom. Like Stephen, Cervantes was intensely interested in literature, particularly in courtly romances, but like Bloom, he was also interested in the economic issues of being a successful writer, and, as exhibited by his hero, he had a first-hand knowledge of the mechanics of printing. These concerns manifested themselves in a form of shameless advertising, with passages in *Don Quixote* plugging Cervantes's own works. For instance, a conversation between the barber and the curate in Book 1, chapter 6 contains the following:

"*La Galatea* of Miguel de Cervantes," said the barber. "Ah, that
fellow Cervantes and I have been friends these many years....
His book has a fairly good plot; it starts out well and ends up
nowhere. We shall have to wait for the second part which he
has promised us, and perhaps when it has been corrected
somewhat it will find the favor that is now denied it."[12] (*DQ* 57)

That Cervantes's personal concerns for the sales of his books
had an unfavorable impact, particularly on Part 2 of *Don Quixote,* has long been the contention of Cervantes scholars. In the
prologue to Part 2, the long harangue regarding Avellaneda's
spurious sequel to Part 1 is self-serving enough, but the continual condemnation throughout the rest of Part 2 does in fact de-
tract from the genius of the work.

The point of this discussion is that there was an eminently
practical, even grubby, side to Cervantes which finds expression
in Sancho's character and which is not unlike that of the old advertising impresario, Bloom, whose concern for art has a decid-
edly commercial cast. If Cervantes's brilliant depiction of Sancho came from some manner of identification with Panza's
character, Joyce — who cared for immortality even more than
for material gain — had an obvious counterpart in Stephen but
had to look for role models for his Ulysses elsewhere among his
acquaintances and in literature. Bloom's marital situation might
have some origins in Joyce's life, but *Exiles* is the work most
closely paralleling the author's own marriage. It is also, in the
opinion of most critics, his most unsuccessful work, chiefly because Joyce identified too closely with the characters and situations to give the play the distance required by those works that
Stephen designates as "dramatic." Lack of distance was certainly
not a problem with *Ulysses.*

The other side of the coin, living life as if it were literature,
is the essence of both *Don Quixote* and *Ulysses.* Both Quixote,
who sets the initial tone of the book and initiates its action, and

Stephen, who performs a comparable role in Joyce's novel, have read too much of the wrong thing, and have predicated their activities and philosophy on literary and symbolic models, confusing life with art. This leads Quixote to hallucinations, or delusions at least, and Stephen to a milder form of delusion, a skewed perspective of people and events. The young Stephen's earlier counterpart in Joyce's fiction, the boy in "Araby," is granted a corrective epiphany to his delusions of courtly love regarding Mangan's sister, but Stephen's reading of *The Count of Monte Cristo* is never mitigated by the rest of his experience in *Portrait*. Such reading is in large part responsible for his vision of the girl on the beach at the end of chapter 4 and the resulting villanelle.

Quixote's principal delusion, the one regarding Dulcinea, is a prime source of his problem with reality throughout the work, as is Stephen's near canonization of E. C., evidence by his continuing emphasis on her in chapter 5 of *Portrait* right through the concluding diary entries. Stephen has doubts about the wisdom of placing his faith in metaphors to determine his course of action after he sees real birds flying around the library steps in place of the archetypal symbols on the beach, where "he *seemed* to hear the noise of dim waves and to see a winged form flying above the waves and slowly climbing the air" (*P* 169; emphasis mine). In the library scene, Stephen admits that "it was folly. But was it for this folly that he was about to leave forever the house of prayer and prudence into which he had been born and the order of life out of which he had come?" (*P* 225).

But Stephen's doubts do not prevail at the end of the book, when he goes "to encounter for the millionth time the *reality* of experience and to forge in the smithy of ... [his] soul the uncreated conscience of ... [his] race (*P* 252–53; emphasis mine). His end is to shape his experience to an artistic didacticism in a quixotic battle with the murky forces and nets of his heritage. In Stephen's defense, he is acting in the mode of his contemporaries in the Irish Literary Revival, who also see literature as an ultimately liberating force. The parallel to *Don Quixote* is striking:

> At last, when his wits were gone beyond repair, he came to conceive the strangest idea that ever occurred to any madman in this world. It now appeared to him fitting and necessary, in order to win a greater amount of honor for himself and serve his country at the same time, to become a knight-errant and roam the world on horseback, in a suit of armor; he would go in quest of adventures, by way of putting into practice all that he had read in his books; he would right every manner of wrong, placing himself in situations of the greatest peril such as would redound to the eternal glory of his name. (*DQ* 27)

By the beginning of *Ulysses,* Stephen has become very adept at applying the events of his own life and society to works of art, as has, we read in Ithaca, his Panza counterpart, Bloom. The seeming convergence of the two figures' philosophies, as we shall presently discuss, also parallels the Quixote-Panza relationship. In the interval between *Portrait* and Telemachus, Stephen's filial relationships have taken on a Shakespearean cast: his ambition to becoming a leader in influencing his country and its literary movement have been thwarted; his idea of history has been colored by Blake; and his whole view of empirical reality has been increasingly influenced by a score of religious and philosophical thinkers. Much of Stephen's universe still derives from books.

Joyce has clearly taken the same premise as Cervantes and given it a more plausible, perhaps more ironic twist, which at first seems more serious than comic, as what purports to be the high road of intellectualism usually does. The comic potential of the situation will be developed early in the novel through the humor generated by that traveler of the low road, Bloom, and later on, as we have seen, by combining both Bloom's and Stephen's adventures with linguistic incongruity.

At the heart of Cervantes's comedy is the interaction of a deluded character, living intellectually in a bygone era, with a group of mundane, occasionally idiosyncratic, but also very realistic characters and events contemporaneous to the narrative present. Hermoine de Almeida has summarized the situation succinctly:

> A mad hidalgo sets forth to realize the ideal of the *caballero andante* in seventeenth-century Spain. Imposing the values of one age on to very different realities of another thus, Cervantes made limitless his subject's potential for artistic play. When they transported Odysseus to range over nineteenth-century Europe and twentieth-century Dublin, Byron and Joyce were attracted by the same possibilities for layered, montaged perspective that the transportation from one age to another would afford. As a novel of the dilemma of a fifty-year-old man who has read too many books, fashioned as a burlesque of epic, pastoral, and romance, *Don Quixote* criticized literature as a whole. In this also it is clear precedent for the Byron and the Joyce who would address the entire literary heritage in *Don Juan* and *Ulysses*.[13]

The deluded protagonists, Quixote and Stephen, translate the activities of their mundane contemporaries into profoundly significant events. Readers in their turn may either extrapolate such actions into another metasignificance or read them as a source of absurd but significant comedy. Clearly the latter is the aim of the present study. In the two books in question, when the principal characters engage in a literary translation of their interaction with their contemporary world, similar to the reader's translation of the novels themselves, the result is a kind of reflexivity akin to literary criticism, with the characters acting as surrogate readers of their own experiences. The product of such an artificial contrivance is often a circular effect in which the absurdity of the act itself becomes meaningful, because the frustrations of the characters parallel the experiences of the readers, who identify with the quest.

The imposition of this sort of illusion-destroying reality is indicative of the reflexive novel and the comic skepticism from which it stems. Robert Alter points out that *Don Quixote,* one of the first works of "the only major genre that comes in to being after the invention of printing, . . . begins out of an erosion of belief in the authority of the written word."[14] Cervantes initially proposed to attack the first popular products of the printing press, chivalric romances. In contriving a series of discussions on the novel as artifice, he set up comic situations which comically condemned the artistic integrity of the very medium he was using.

However, Cervantes's purpose of debunking the literature of chivalry and the codes that go with it by its end ironically heightens the notoriety of the very code the author sought to debunk. The strength of Quixote's convictions causes the other characters, even in their incessant baiting of him, to assume the roles he has created for them. In short, the world changes to fit his image of it. When just before he dies he returns to his senses, his friends strive mightily to perpetuate his earlier delusions, which seem preferable to the new delusions of realism into which they fear he has fallen.

Cervantes started a comic genre in which illusion and realism were at war, in terms of both the medium of presentation and the actions the fiction describes. Joyce followed in the same path by setting up Stephen's illusions and Bloom's comic antidote as the fictions of *Ulysses,* and then later in the novel by distorting the verisimilitude of his fictions with nonrealistic comic language. As a result, *Ulysses,* like *Don Quixote,* paradoxically reaffirms humanity.

Cervantes's ultimate portrayal of a man's striving to provide a meaning for existence is normally the essence of tragedy, but is nearly inseparable from the comic view of reality afforded by what we think of as common sense. The convergence of comic and tragic is at the heart of the ultimate conjunction of Sancho and Quixote, and of Stephen and Bloom. That two such different characters in Joyce's novel, while displaying polemically different mind-sets, should evince some sort of commonality could hardly have been accidental, as it might well have been in *Don Quixote*. *Ulysses* explores the parameters of commonality in the father-son theme, the artistic creation motif, and the parallel metaphors of religious identity (transubstantiation-consubstantiation) and physical identity (parallax).

If comedy thrives on incongruity, the juxtaposition of apparent opposites, its end is an accommodation to a seemingly chaotic universe brought into harmony through artistic means. Thus, as de Almeida says, *Don Quixote* and *Ulysses* are, among other things, both books about literary criticism. Both explore the ideas of literature as opposed to those of the "real" world, and both contain long discussions of individual literary works. While *Don Quixote* parodies principally epic, pastoral, and romantic forms, *Ulysses* concentrates on a literary parody of the same archetypal epic from which it draws its name, and at the same time mocks all the literary styles which it emulates in the later chapters.

In *Don Quixote* Cervantes provides a trickster figure to counter the Don's delusions. When the witty Bachelor Sanson Carrasco, recently a student at Salamanca, has his initial meeting with Quixote, his treatment of the Don is laced with mockery and sarcasm, as Carrasco throws himself at Quixote's feet professing a profound respect for the Don's delusions. The Bachelor's plan, unswerving throughout the book, is to best the Don at his own game, and finally to rid Quixote of his delusions or chivalric pretensions, at the same time having fun at the Don's expense. The Bachelor is intelligent and as utterly convinced of the rightness of his own mind-set as he is of the Don's folly.

He appears first to Quixote clad in cleric's garb, though his concerns, both in school and out, seem to be with the secular rather than with the divine. Like most trickster figures, he is a chameleon, using disguises to bring about the Don's downfall. Although he appears to have Quixote's best interests at heart, his defeat of the Don on the field of battle and Quixote's resulting oath to refrain from any more adventures for a year bring an end to the Don's dream, and, if they are not directly responsible for his death, are assumed by the characters to have a lot to do with it. Viewed uncharitably, the Bachelor could be deemed a usurper, a jealous rival, whose sole purpose in the novel is to bring Quixote low and destroy his dream. That aspect we can only conjecture, for, like those of Panurge and all trickster figures, Carrasco's motives and essence remain shadowy.

The obvious counterpart in *Ulysses* is Buck Mulligan. An acknowledged student-wit, he appears to Stephen in mock clerical robes, flattering, cajoling, and systematically destroying the delusions on which Stephen has posited his existence. Performing his own little black mass, Mulligan parodies Stephen's vision of himself as high priest of art "transmuting [through his art] the daily bread of experience into the radiant body of everliving life" (*P* 221). Mulligan proceeds to attack Stephen's Dedalean rationalizations by offering to join him in Hellenizing Ireland, and then by rendering Buck's comic "Ballad of Joking Jesus," in which all of Stephen's bird imagery is debunked along with its Christian counterparts. Finally, after rubbing a sensitive nerve by evoking the image of Stephen's dying mother, Mulligan elaborates Stephen's latest literary folly by telling Haines, "He proves by algebra that Hamlet's grandson is Shakespeare's grandfather and that he himself is the ghost of his own father" (*U* 1:555 – 56; 1961:18). Like Carrasco's, Mulligan's motives are suspect. While Stephen has not totally succumbed to his own literary fictions (he admits in the library that he does not believe his own theory), he is clearly casting about for literary precedents on which to frame his actions and rationale for life. Mulligan won't cause the end of Stephen's dreams, as Carrasco did the Don's, but the rivalry is unmistakable and the label *usurper* here seems as justified to the reader as it does to Stephen.

Clearly Mulligan does not permanently disenchant Stephen, who shortly thereafter in rebuttal transforms a milkwoman into a symbol of Ireland. Stephen is seldom depicted as a comic butt the way Quixote was, though Stephen's Quixotic adventures extend at least through Circe, where, in Bella Cohen's, he breaks a chandelier which he has mistaken for his dead mother's evil specter. Following this incident, in typical Quixotic fashion he takes on Privates Carr and Compton, addressing them in a formal language, which beggars their understanding and eventually leads them to give him the sort of trouncing habitual with Quixote during his perambulations.

All of this occurs in an episode in which the dreamlike quality of the action is apparent. It epitomizes the delusions of the principal characters by objectifying Bloom's aspirations and fears and by literally depicting and thus debunking such delusions of Stephen's as the Shakespearean theory. When the mirror image of Bloom and Stephen is transformed into Shakespeare's nonsense-babbling visage, a comic corrective deprives the theory of its last vestiges of believability. Circe is certainly one of the funniest chapters of the novel, mostly because the projections of Stephen and Bloom's posturings are so incongruous as to be comical. Bloom's rise to Messiahship and his subsequent fall, for instance, more than rival any of Panza's grandiose prognostications for his future as a leader.

In *Don Quixote* the counterpart to the Circean dream world is the Don's dream in the Cave of Montesinos, an episode which, far from debunking the Don's hallucinations, almost provides a bridge between the realistic contemporary world and the idealistic dreamworld of the Don's projections. The twentieth-century Joyce was not to be lulled into any tidy conclusions such as are present in the last chapter of *Don Quixote*.

Both novels were rightly accused of having a certain random quality about them. Cervantes switched narrators and used his novel to host a long collection of miscellaneous stories, poetry, literary criticism, and so forth, in the long-standing tradition of haphazardness in comic narrative fiction. The seemingly random disconnectedness of the stories within the novel certainly had its antecedents in *The Arabian Nights*, Boccaccio, and Chaucer. Cervantes, like Sterne, was working in a basic mode of comedy, which depends in large measure on arbitrariness and the disconcertion of order. Cervantes was said to have come upon his masterpiece accidentally, with his novel growing into greatness as it progressed.[15]

Likewise Joyce is said to have abandoned his original design along with the "initial" narrative style eleven chapters into his book. The harshest interpretation of this was that *Ulysses* was fatally flawed because the linguistic pyrotechnics of the later chapters had little to do with the artistic intent of the earlier ones. The technique of comic writing, however, embraces a frustration of convention, as we have seen in the chapter on language. The same holds true for any sort of incongruities the author incorporates into his work. Conventions and traditions have always been fair game for comic writers, whose form dictates the confounding of normal expectations. For instance, in the same manner as the characters in Part 2 of *Don Quixote* discuss themselves as the characters of Part 1, the later chapters of *Ulysses* — Circe and Ithaca especially — provide ironic, sometimes satiric, but always comic commentary on the motifs, characters, and scenes in the first half of the book.

Cervantes began his book as an ultimate realist, fell in love with a human frailty capable of being deluded by the outmoded code he was trying to debunk, and concluded with a statement about the power of human endurance. Joyce, too, began *Ulysses* as an ultimate realist, ironically portraying the goals Stephen exposed, which, mirrored in the comic character of Bloom, take on a new cast and lead to a concluding comic endorsement of man's struggles with his own existence.

The Don's seemingly ridiculous defence of his belief in Dulcinea early in Part 1 of *Don Quixote* becomes by the end of Part 2 the very inspiration we take from the novel: "If I were to show her to you . . . what merit would there be in your confessing a truth so self-evident? The important thing is for you, without seeing her, to believe, confess, affirm, swear, and defend that truth" (*DQ* 45). Comedy and tragedy are alternative methods at arriving at truth. The high road to this end starts out with some spiritual value-laden hypothesis, and, regardless of whether it defies prudence or reason (i.e., Antigone's adherence to burial rituals, or Orestes' adherence to the revenge pattern), pursues the idea through a tragic revelation of the ultimate good. To take the low road is to start out lacking any belief in a higher order of values, and, being principally concerned with one's own well-being, to pursue the ends of comfort, pleasure, and monetary gain, which may or may not be granted by the end of the work. If these ends are not achieved it is of comparatively little consequence in a comedy, since the spiritual stakes are so low. At least in a comedy, although the protagonists may not get what they want, they don't usually die.

Comedies usually contain an underlying sense of normal order, perhaps unrecognized at the beginning, which is the result of the characters' live-and-let-live approach to life and which will ultimately evidence itself. In the comic as in the tragic world there is a satisfying rightness to things, no matter how stupid, chaotic, or frustrating they appear to be at the moment.

The convergence of the high and low roads provides the ultimate structure of both *Don Quixote* and *Ulysses*. Leopold Bloom is, as we have seen, the Sancho Panza of *Ulysses*. The Don's description of Sancho might well apply to Bloom:

He is so sharp in his simple-mindedness that one may derive no little amusement from trying to determine whether he is in reality simple or sharp-witted. He has in him a certain malicious streak that seems to indicate he is a rogue, and from his blundering you would take him for a dunce. He doubts everything and believes everything, and just as I think he is about to tumble headlong, owing to some stupidity, he will come up with some witticism or other that sends him skyward in my estimation. (*DQ* 725)

Bloom shares innumerable traits with his seventeenth-century counterpart, from a keen appetite for peasant food (the first we hear of him is that he "ate with relish the inner organs of beasts and fowls" [*U* 4:1–2; 1961:55]), through a general concern for the well-being of his digestive system, to his flatulence. According to Bakhtin, Sancho and, by extension, Bloom participate in a comic heritage dating to antiquity:

Sancho's fat belly *(panza),* his appetite and thirst still convey a powerful carnivalesque spirit. His love of abundance and wealth have not, as yet, a basically private, egotistic and alienating character. Sancho is the direct heir of the antique potbellied demons which decorate the famous Corinthian vases. In Cervantes' images of food and drink there is still the spirit of popular banquets. Sancho's materialism, his potbelly, appetite, his abundant defecation, are on the absolute lower level of grotesque realism of the gay bodily grave (belly, bowels, earth) which has been dug for Don Quixote's abstract and deadened idealism.[16]

The same might be said for Bloom's earthiness as the burial place for Stephen's deadened abstractions, in a rebirth of comic vitality.

Bloom and Sancho have more in common than their digestive systems and economic concerns. They each have wives who pride themselves on their own commonsense view of life. When Teresa admonishes Sancho, "Don't dispute my word ... I talk the way God would have me talk without beating around the bush" (*DQ* 543), the words might well have come from Molly.

The initial aims of neither Panza or Bloom are especially high. They both want to make money, and, without thinking it possible, want to be the rulers of their respective islands. Their social outlooks are very similar. Both are a bit extraordinary, even bizarre, in their solutions to the problems of their lives and societies, as well as those of the constituents of their mythical domains; however, their social and legal schemes have a zany logic which borders on genius, and their potential justice and even-handedness as rulers bespeak the fundamental decency of their philosophy.

When they meet their misguided inspirational figures, they both develop delusions of wealth and grandeur, Sancho as governor of an island, Bloom as musical impresario. When pushed by circumstances both rise above themselves to acts and speeches approaching heroism, but the principal roles for each are to provide the low, comic correspondences to their Quixotic counterparts. As Cervantes's curate tells us, "It would seem they [Quixote and Panza] had both been turned out from the same mold and that the madness of the master without the foolishness of the man would not be worth a penny" (*DQ* 522). It is easy enough to see how the Don's chivalric quests are countered by Sancho's greedy ones, and how the dream of Dulcinea has its parallel in Sancho's wife, Teresa, and so forth. In contrast, the correspondences between specific motifs established by Stephen and by Bloom are not so apparent.

In both books the Quixote characters make their appearances first and establish the primary motifs of the novels: Quixote's discontent with his contemporary world, and his wish to establish a new identity derived from his books; and Stephen's problems with his mother and Ireland, and his need to establish a new identity through another literary aesthetic. Sancho Panza is introduced in chapter 7 after Quixote has already been out on his first sally and returned, just as Bloom appears in the fourth episode of *Ulysses,* after Stephen has already met his class and strolled along the beach. The clock is turned back for Bloom's introduction, but not before Stephen in Proteus reaffirms the motifs begun in Telemachus, while at the same time emphasizing the all-encompassing theme of transformation.

During the last ten years Joyce scholars have increasingly recognized the importance of transformation as perhaps the major concept of *Ulysses.*[17] In a way Joyce's adaptation of the *Odyssey* is built upon transforming the archetypal hero of Western civilization into a Dublin cuckold-ad salesman. The making of literature itself, as Stephen stresses in the last chapter of *Portrait,* involves a transformation process akin to the priest's transubstantiation of wine and wafer. The theme is taken up again in the first pages of *Ulysses* and elaborated on with a host of other transformation motifs (Shakespeare's composition of *Hamlet* from the details of his own life, consubstantiation, the link between fathers and sons, etc.). In Proteus, it is further expanded with philosophical and theological underpinnings, such as the references to Lessing, the Platonists, Aristotle, the ecclesiastical heresies, and a host of philosophical and natural phenomena.

Shortly after Bloom is introduced in Calypso, he is involved in a parallel transformation motif, growing out of Molly's question about *metempsychosis.* Such allied phenomena as transmigration of souls and reincarnation are offered in Bloom's answer, which is further expanded to include a series of mundane peripheral items like the nymph's picture over the bed, and *Ruby: The Pride of the Ring.* Bloom is Panza-izing Stephen's motif. Later Bloom's preoccupation with the scientific, empirical parallel phenomenon of parallax adds another worldly dimension to the essential nature of the motif. There are of course scores of permutations of the theme on both Bloom's and Stephen's sides throughout the novel. For purposes of this discussion, however, I wish to concentrate on the transformation that apparently blends the minds of Bloom and Stephen, a movement that emulates the converging ideas of Quixote and Panza.

In the first place, I am not convinced that Stephen's mind is any closer philosophically or intellectually to Bloom's at the end of the novel than it was at the outset. Neither has Panza's basic philosophy changed. Despite Quixote's death, Panza is much comforted by his share of the inheritance from his master. Panza may no longer wish to be governor of an island, but that is because the job is harder and more spartan than he thought it would be and there is no money to speak of in the enterprise. The moral aspects of Panza's character, though refined by his association with the Don, remain basically similar to his master's. The circumstances of the plot merely develop these similarities. All of the characters who humor Quixote at the end of Part 2 fundamentally believe in the moral integrity that he espouses, but are certainly not, though they may profess otherwise, deluded into thinking that they live in chivalric times.

Similarly, the seeming convergence of Stephen and Bloom does not represent any great philosophic reversals on their parts, but rather the reader's recognition that they are really concerned about similar things, which, while appearing initially to be of widely different origin, become more apparently aspects of the same ideas as the novel develops. The comedy stems from the seeming incongruity of the high and and low approaches to the concepts and events that form the basis of the action. While Stephen is not as deluded as Quixote, nor Bloom as simple-minded as Sancho, the two modern protagonists do represent those high and low approaches of the earlier characters in almost everything they think and do. Let me develop just a few of the comic contrasts between Bloom and Stephen.

The way in which they regard women is a case in point. Stephen, while less concerned with the subject in *Ulysses*, has not abandoned his habit of regarding them as archetypal, symbolic figures, such as Virgin, temptress, inspiration figure — the girl on the beach in *Portrait* being a prime example. Bloom's girl on the beach is Gerty MacDowell, whose thoughts are far from being of the ethereal nature projected by Stephen on his idealized bird-girl. Bloom's reaction is not like Stephen's self-induced intellectual orgasm, which used Donne's "The Ecstasy" as a prophylactic, but is a literal orgasm produced by physical manipulation. When Stephen sees the drawers of the gazing girl, he gets his thrill by transforming them into bird feathers; when Bloom sees Gerty's pants, he literally takes matters in hand and masturbates. If Bloom calls up any vision at the time, it is of the cuckolding Molly. The spiritual E. C. of the concluding chapter of *Portrait* is replaced in *Ulysses* by Molly, whose goddess-like image on the chamber pot concludes the novel. Stephen might aspire to take the dull, gross voice of common experience and transform it into inspirational art, but Joyce transforms spiritual posturing into elimination to produce a higher comic art.

Bloom's literalism constantly leads him to investigate the physical aspects of ideas that Stephen regards only in spiritual, philosophical, or inspirational terms. Bloom, unsatisfied with the symbolic import of the goddesses, will check the museum to find out whether they were conceived by the sculptor as having all their natural orifices. Where Stephen will close his eyes to speculate on the relationship of color to natural objects, Bloom will put his hand inside his shirt to finger his navel in order to discover whether a blind man can recognize that his own belly button is yellow.

Stephen conceives of artistic creation as taking place in an atmosphere approaching Dante's vision of God: "This supreme quality is felt by the artist when the esthetic image is first conceived in his imagination. The mind in that mysterious instant Shelley likened beautifully to a fading coal. The instant wherein that supreme quality of beauty, the clear radiance of the esthetic image, is apprehended luminously by the mind which has been arrested by its wholeness and fascinated by its harmony is the luminous silent stasis of esthetic pleasure" (*P* 213). There is, it was said, a bit of the artist in old Bloom. His first thoughts of creating something in the artistic line occur to him in the jakes, as he reads Philip Beaufoy's prize titbit and contemplates the payment received. Art and life coalesce in Bloom's production: "Quietly he read, restraining himself, the first column and, yielding but resisting, began the second. Midway, his last resistance yielding, he allowed his bowels to ease themselves quietly as he read, reading still patiently that slight constipation of yesterday quite gone. Hope it's not too big bring on piles again. No, just right. So. Ah! Costive. One tabloid of cascara sagrada. Life might be so. It did not move or touch him but it was something quick and neat" (*U* 4:506–12; 1961:69).

Bloom is indeed arrested by the wholeness and fascinated by the harmony of his humble production, achieving a stasis of aesthetic pleasure from the act. The epiphany lies in comic commonality between the Bloomian and Dedalean points of view, and the possibility that the metaphoric transformation of gold into base metal may in fact result in the creation of a far more valuable artistic substance. When Bloom associates his creation with Beaufoy's by wiping himself with the prize story, he accords Beaufoy a comic immortality far greater than the *Titbits* readership could ever provide. When the specter of Beaufoy rises in Circe to condemn Bloom for disfiguring Beaufoy's maturer work with the hallmark of the beast, it might well be Joyce's way of addressing critics like Beaufoy who accuse him of a cloacal obsession. As Crazy Jane observed, "Fair needs foul," and ideology requires a comic corrective.

Bakhtin saw this tendency of "popular-festive merriment"

as a pattern of descent images toward truth and the sublime by way of the lower body and its functions: "Finally, debasement is the fundamental artistic principle of grotesque realism: all that is sacred and exalted is rethought on the level of the material bodily stratum or else combined and mixed with its images. We spoke of the grotesque swing, which brings together heaven and earth. But the accent is placed not on the upward movement but on the descent."[18] Ultimately, truth is at the bottom of things.

Another major theme in which Quixote, Panza, Bloom, and Stephen all participate is the Messianic motif. Quixote and Stephen would save the world by changing its reading habits: Quixote would restore the chivalric codes, while Stephen would write new ones. Sancho's governorship reveals his fairness, common sense, and humanity, while Bloom's potential for positive leadership emerges from his social schemes, his efforts and donation for Dignam's family, as well as his concern for Mrs. Purefoy, Mrs. Breen, and Stephen, and his willingness to espouse a philosophy of love in a barroom atmosphere uncongenial to the doctrine.

One difference between Sancho's apparent realization of his dreams and the Circe projection of the New Bloomusalem is that the comic situations set up by the Duke for Sancho to display his clownishness backfire in a sense, because Panza turns out far wiser than anyone had thought. While Bloom descends as rapidly as he rises, his schemes during his Circe elevation are even whackier and funnier than the ones he contemplates during the day. The preponderant comedy of Circe stems from its exaggeration of events, hints, impulses, and objects occurring earlier in the novel.

Stephen's Messiahship stems from his idea of forging in the smithy of his soul the uncreated conscience of his race. The aim was not so different from that of other Irish Renaissance writers. It also hints at the martyrdom associated with Irish patriots and with Christ. Both of these elements are present in

Telemachus when Stephen remembers his conversations with Patrice Egan, who is going to send Stephen Taxil's *La Vie de Jesus*. The Christian motif is of course associated with the father-son motif, which in turn is linked to the *Hamlet* theme in a never-ending cycle. Of the scores of themes critics have discovered intertwined through *Ulysses*, most have counterparts in the thoughts and activities of both Bloom and Stephen.

The question arises, then, whether the parallel or shared motifs of Bloom and Stephen effect any eventual common identification, consubstantiation, metempsychic congruence, or anything of the sort. I used to think so, but now I am much less Quixotic in my projections.[19] What Joyce indicates is that most men, no matter what their status in life, address similar problems, have analogous aspirations, suffer matching humiliations and defeats, and enjoy occasional corresponding successes. Joyce certainly enjoyed the comic potential of the interchangeability of Stoom and Blephen in their comparison of ancestral languages, hopes, fears, ages, and sizes, but the nature of the comedy itself leads to the impression that conclusive definitions of identity may not be forthcoming. I don't think they ever arrive.

The metamorphosis of Quixote from madman to tragic, pitiful protagonist was the mistake of a comic writer eager to kill his hero off to keep the imitators from making money off him. The real comic import of the book didn't need that, and I don't think Joyce was ready to make the same mistake. If anything, he did his best to avoid any tragic sentimentality. He knew such sentiment was lurking in the hearts of loyal readers who had followed him through seven hundred uncharted pages of the second most difficult literary terrain ever crossed, but he still retained enough of Ibsen's antisentimental influence to make it difficult for readers to reconcile the realism and common sense of comedy with the pathos of tragic significance.

The multiplicity of motifs, indeed the encyclopedic nature

of *Don Quixote* and *Ulysses,* is facilitated by the episodic nature of the structure of both works. Borrowing their framework from the Odyssean tales of the road, in which episodes and events are singular enough to stand as comparable entities, yet are closely enough associated by the frame story to be considered part of the same fabric, Cervantes and Joyce composed masterpieces of comic irrelevance. The particular comic nature of the two books owes much to their Odyssean predecessor, for both books are about public activities, the interaction of the protagonists with a series of seemingly unrelated random citizens: cross sections of early seventeenth-century Spain and turn-of-the-century Ireland. Like *The Canterbury Tales,* they are books about eras as seen through the comic idiosyncracies of individuals who are both part of a collective society and at the same time unique.

Normalcy is the backdrop against which the comic quirks and incongruities of the characters are played out. Thus, Chaucer's tales can collectively be deemed a panorama of medieval life, while at the same time they present some of the most individualistic characters in literature. Epics have a multitude of characters and epic roll calls, but comedies such as *Don Quixote* and *Ulysses,* equally swelled by large casts and mock-epic roll calls, paint far larger panoramas, with their exaggeration, eccentricities, and commonality.

STERNE

The parallels between *Tristram Shandy* and *Ulysses* are not as immediately striking as those between Joyce and Cervantes because they are less involved with character and situation than with technique. Although all great comic writers made unique contributions to the art, as the tradition grew there was more to imitate, so that a diligent and inventive critic may see as derivative even those instances where the author made no attempt to emulate his precursors. Lodwick Hartley warns against placing too much emphasis upon similarities between Sterne and Joyce:

"Merely superficial resemblances and allusions should not be allowed to argue for a more fundamental relationship than actually existed."[20] Since form, structure, and style have a more subjective nature than the empirical activities of characters, this critic at least is wary of identifying Sterne as the source of any of the compositional innovations of *Ulysses;* however, similarities abound, and even dissimilarities prove useful in making the case for *Ulysses* as a comic novel.

In *Ulysses* Joyce was less precise in his identification of his comic predecessors' influence than was Sterne in his continual direct references in *Tristram Shandy* to Rabelais and more especially to *Don Quixote.* Coupled with Joyce's lack of direct allusions to Sterne is an apparent difficulty in drawing any specific detailed character analogies between the casts of the *Ulysses* and *Tristram Shandy.* We must turn instead to structure and technique to look for major sources of similarity.

Ann Ridgeway, the first Joyce scholar to treat at any length Sterne's influence on *Ulysses,* is also one of the first to see Joyce as predominantly a comic novelist: "Both authors work with a script of fundamentally high comedy. The satire in Sterne's novel is directed toward so many of the same human foibles which are the data of Joyce's work that I think of both books as examples of a sort of comedy of bourgeois manners."[21] The point is that the common techniques she saw are principally used by both authors as the vehicles for a comic overview of life. Among the shared techniques Ridgeway enumerated are that Joyce and Sterne both break from rigid chronological narrative; both use the stream-of-consciousness technique; both "combine a variety of musical devices with more or less elaborate literary allusion and word play"; and "both record the trivia of everyday life in exploring the universals of human experience: birth, death, sexual behavior, psychological normality and abnormality, sensitivity and sensibility, and the continual frustration of goals not quite attained."[22]

I would like to elaborate on these selected parallels for a

moment, first to say that Joyce's use of the techniques mentioned varies considerably from Sterne's. For example, Sterne's dedication is delayed until chapter 8, following which he offers to sell it to the highest bidder, and his preface does not appear until Book 3, chapter 20. Joyce marched through the day in chronological order, right enough, stepping out of sequence only in turning back the clock to begin Bloom's day at the same time he began Stephen's. What appear to be disconcertions of time occur during the second half of *Ulysses,* where the narrative elaborations slow the chronology of the actions depicted. Time apparently stands still in Circe, but the Circe clock runs on subconscious time, more in the tradition of Goethe's Brocken Mountain than Shandy Hall. What Joyce and Sterne share here is the comic legacy of Rabelais, the disconcerting of normal expectations through digressions, which because they appear to be endless and because they offer such self-conscious deviations from the normal time sequence expected, appear funny, producing a shaggy-dog-story kind of comedy. A case in point is Slop's hilariously extended damning of Obadiah, which goes on for eight pages in both English and Latin.

Sterne not only incorporated such digressions as the long peroration on why Tristram's mother was not a papist, but also long digressive disquisitions on his use of digressions: "Digressions, incontestably, are the sunshine; — they are the life, the soul of reading;—take them out of this book for instance,—you might as well take the book along with them;—one cold eternal winter would reign in every page of it; restore them to the writer;—he steps forth like a bridegroom,—bids All hail; brings in variety, and forbids the appetite to fail"[23] (*TS* 62–63). What makes this particularly funny, aside from the concluding simile, is that it appears as yet another in a series of incongruous digressions. By itself it might easily be considered a slightly hyperbolic but rational opinion on narrative chronology.

Joyce's digression, such as the Cyclops' roll calls, the Circe processions, the contents of dresser drawers at Number Seven, and the tedious exploration of various positions on irrelevancies during Ithaca, are all equally comic because of their very disconcertation of expected narrative chronology and relevance. The action seems to stop, or at least slow to a crawl. Joyce's intent here is closer to Sterne than to Rabelais. By calling attention to the artificiality of the novel itself, Joyce introduces a realistic point of view, which is at the heart of the comic art, inviting us to refrain from pity and fear and enjoy. When Dorothy Van Ghent tells us that "in reading *Tristram Shandy*, we are never allowed to forget that the activity of creation, as an activity of forming perceptions and maneuvering them into an expressive order, *is itself the subject*," she might well be talking about *Ulysses*.[24] In the first half of the book we get the artistic rationale from Stephen, and in the second half, by disconcerting the expectations raised by the first half, we get the theory put into unverbalized but eloquent comic practice.

Further, the vehicle of most of Sterne's digressions is the mind of the first-person narrator himself, whose associative patterns cause a disruption of the plot by inserting opinions and actions more immediately important to him than those which would traditionally develop the action. The humor again lies in the incongruity of the reader's thwarted expectations. The comic fiction stems from the verisimilitude of Tristram, the putative author, in letting us know that what he gives us are his own opinions about his life, and not a contrived fiction. That the whole business is precisely a contrivance is the comic conundrum.

Joyce's digressions have much the same aim: comically to disconcert the reader, and to defamiliarize normal or serious plot expectations. The result is a degree of reflexivity which has led many critics to assert that Joyce is really engaging, as did his comic predecessors, in acts of literary criticism. One aspect of the digression technique that Sterne and Joyce did not owe to

Rabelais is that their seemingly irrelevant details and motifs come back later to haunt the faithful reader with echoes, elaborations, and relevance to future actions. Bloom's Dodd anecdote, the potato, and Agendath Netaim all strut and fret their moment upon the stage, and then are resurrected in the next act as important motifs.

Although both Sterne and Joyce used stream of consciousness, Sterne's vehicle was an extended first-person narrative, while Joyce used, and for comparatively brief episodes, only two first-person narrators, the Cyclops barfly and Molly, among a host of third-person narrative voices. Couple this with the fact that nearly 150 years of new theories and literature had flowed beneath the psychological bridge, and the differences between Sterne's and Joyce's stream-of-consciousness techniques become more apparent. While *Tristram Shandy* repeatedly acknowledges Sterne's debt to Locke's *Essay Concerning Human Understanding*, *Ulysses* pays no such obeisance to Sterne, Locke, Bergson, Freud, Jung, Proust, or any of the others who developed mental associative patterns as narrative vehicles. In shunning narrative artifice as subject for conscious discussion by the narrators of *Ulysses*, Joyce prevented the book from becoming wholly the reflexive novel that *Tristram Shandy* was. Instead we occasionally enter such diverse minds as Bloom's, Stephen's, Molly's, Dignam's son's, and Father Conmee's without ever being afforded the least grounds for the suspicion (which we had to some degree in *Portrait*) that we are privy to the thoughts of the author himself, or that he is presenting a chorus character who is debating the merits of the construct of his own work. By 1922 the stream-of-consciousness technique was no longer disconcerting enough to be funny in its own right, and thus the main source of the humor derived from the technique is the incongruity of some of the characters' free associations.

The subliminal world of Circe, one of the funniest episodes in the novel, is another matter. While Joyce was indebted to Goethe and writers other than Sterne for this tradition, Joyce turned the normally sinister dark side of the mind into something more comic than it was frightening. The normal reaction to our unconscious is to be afraid of it, since it lacks the restraints of either superego or social decorum. If Joyce's projections are to be perceived as having any sort of validity, man is not merely the rapine-wreaking, violently aggressive bundle of neuroses we all are terrified to confront, but rather, as exemplified by Bloom, a comic exaggeration of the fears and aspirations we experience in our conscious minds every day. That is to say, if Joyce's perception of the conscious world is comic, then his depiction of the subconscious world is hilarious.

In Circe Joyce was able to push comic indecorousness to new heights, or lows, depending on your point of view. Stephen's interaction with the subconscious world is largely a terrifying guilt experience for him, concluding with the climactic *"ruin of all space, shattered glass and toppling masonry"* (*U* 15:4245; 1961:583) after he breaks the chandelier, but Bloom conversely gets a sense of masochistic pleasure from the projected climactic copulation of Blazes and Molly. The counterpart to Stephen's fantasized massive destruction occurs when Bloom's trousers' button snaps. The response of the button to Bloom's catastrophe is a comic "Bip!" (*U* 15:3441; 1961:552) just as the response of the gasjet to Stephen's Armageddon is "Pwfungg!" (*U* 15:4247; 1961:583)

In Circe, as elsewhere in the book, the fantasies involving Bloom play a comic counterpoint to the Quixotic ones involving Stephen. If the external events of Dublin life in 1904 are basically comic in nature, it stands to reason that the exaggerations of the subconscious world should be even funnier. The heritage of Virag, whose presence in Circe might have been construed as potentially threatening, is the advice of a libidinous old lecher, the traditional stuff of comedy. Like the Cyclops episode, Circe provided a plausible prime opportunity for Joyce to develop a tragic or melodramatic situation with serious overtones. Instead, he chose to mitigate that seriousness with comic narration in Cyclops and comic projections in Circe.

Ridgeway's point that Joyce and Sterne use abundant literary allusion and wordplay might be said of a majority of writers of high comedy. Here again the differences between Sterne and Joyce are as significant as the characteristics they share. Sterne's literary allusions are often provided by the narrator, and the overabundance of the characters' references to literary works for guidance to their own activities is a recurrent comic motif. The humor of Walter and Toby's hauling out volumes to check precedents for current events and the formulation or confirmation of their opinions increases with each new instance in *Tristram Shandy*. It is not so apparent at the outset of *Ulysses* that Stephen's opinions and courses of actions follow the comic road of Rabelais, Cervantes, and Sterne. The three earlier writers begin with comic protagonists and do not initially need the idiosyncracies of a Panurge, Panza, or Toby to establish comic credentials for their enterprises. Stephen Dedalus, however, is not perceived either in the beginning or end as principally a comic character, and Joyce's dependence on Bloom to provide a comic counterpoint is paramount. Stephen's use of literary allusion, discussed earlier in detail, sets motifs to be comically augmented directly by Bloom's references to Shakespeare and indirectly by analogous opinions and situations. Besides the allusions to literary works by a number of characters, including D. B. Murphy, Joyce made indirect allusions through his use of all of the narrative parodies of the later chapters, as the novel took on an increasingly comic import.

Wordplay, while admittedly present in Joyce, is not so obvious a comic technique in *Ulysses* as parody, at least not in the earlier episodes. Self-conscious intrusions such as dashes, asterisks, and omissions, which were more common in the eighteenth-century novel than in the twentieth, are a staple of *Tris-*

tram Shandy, but are only sprinkled comparatively unobtrusively through the early chapters of *Ulysses.* There is little to claim our undivided attention until the addition of the headlines in Aeolus. Thereafter, idiosyncracies, chiefly parodic, abound.

Ridgeway's observation that both Sterne and Joyce record the trivia of everyday life to get at universal human experience calls our attention to a feature that was central to the earlier novel (we certainly waited long enough for Tristram's birth), and one that became increasingly important as *Ulysses* progressed. We are held up by the elaborate description of Simon's high B flat at the end of *"M'appari"* and by the tangential ceremonies described by the second narrator of Cyclops, but the situation does not become acutely comic until we are hampered by the clichés of Eumaeus and the comically painful elucidations of Ithaca. In both *Ulysses* and *Tristram Shandy* (where we shift our attention from Tristram's birth to the nature of Uncle Toby's wound and its relation to his affair with the Widow Wadman) we become more desperate for answers as the books draw to their conclusions. We know Toby didn't marry the widow, so our attention rivets on the relationship between Toby's wound and why his proposal was either withdrawn or rejected. When in response to the Widow's question about where the wound was inflicted, Toby produces detailed maps and charts to indicate the precise geographical location, our laughter stems as much from our frustration as from Toby's innocence.

Our increasingly desperate search for answers in Ithaca about the relation between Bloom and Stephen runs into similar comic frustration. The right questions produce the wrong answers, the seemingly irrelevant questions, tantalizing but insufficient answers, and so we shift our attention to the final absurdity: whether Molly will serve Bloom's breakfast in bed the next morning. So nebulous is our hold on any final conclusive truth to be drawn from the nonmomentous events of Bloomsday that Joyce invites us to roll the universe into a ball and ask the overwhelming question: Did Molly's "yes" mean she would in fact fry his bacon on the seventeenth? I, for one, am glad I'll never know. "The continual frustration of goals not quite obtained," to which Ridgeway refers, pertains to the reader as well as the characters. When many, perhaps most, comedies end in a life lived happily ever after, readers are asked to accept a convention that they know to be untrue in the light of comic realism. What they really assume is that life goes on, with all its foibles, frustrations, and uncertainty. By not asserting an unequivocally happy resolution, Sterne and Joyce protected us from the contradictions of the comic tradition, while they used what it had to offer.

As I stated previously, any comparison between the characterization techniques of Sterne and Joyce is likely to bear less fruit than between compositional ones. Still, something may profitably be said about their respective characters as a part of the comic tradition. Sterne was closer to the comic norm in presenting his characters essentially as caricatures, with dominant foibles, humors, hobbyhorses, or preoccupations. Since predictability is part of the comic rhythm, we expect Uncle Toby to respond to any situation with military metaphors. The comic incongruity lies in an essentially gentle nature enamored with the artifacts of war. Walter Shandy's responses to events are similarly shaped by the analogies he draws to literary works, and the brothers' tweedledum-tweedledee reactions provide much of the humor of the novel. For example, the fact that Walter regards sex as a part of his marital obligations, to be punctually performed like winding the clock, supplies the book's initial comic situation. The brothers have, like all caricatures, chosen quaint but unrealistic rationales to cope with the realistic events of the world around them. Knowing these predispositions, the audience can derive pleasure by anticipating their reactions to external events. We see such situations in Cervantes, and in the works of such diverse caricature creators as Dickens and Dostoevski.

Joyce's characters in *Ulysses* were another matter. For all
Stephen's idiosyncrasies, we do not see him governed by any delusion to the point of comic predictability. He was never a caricature of the artist as a young man, any more than Bloom is a
Madison Avenue type. As with the Shandys, the reactions of
Bloom and Stephen to sex are among the most mirth-provoking
character traits in the book. The Shandys are forced to confront
their ineffectuality and are humbled by women's roles in birth.
They are forced to sit downstairs pontificating on a broad range
of literary analogies which lead them off into other comforting
digressions. Walter's insistence on the male Slop's presence results in Tristram's nose being crushed with Slop's forceps.

In Oxen of the Sun, one of the most Shandyesque episodes
of *Ulysses*, the medical students chauvinistically confine most of
their banter on the subject of birth to the male role in insemi-
nation, while Stephen draws comparisons between birthing and
literary and heavenly creation, obliquely seeing himself as the
central figure in the process. The whole scene is couched in the
literatures of antiquity, colored by the idiosyncratic points of
view of scores of narrators and a general insensitivity to what is
taking place upstairs. Only Bloom, the new womanly man, demonstrates any concern with Mrs. Purefoy or appreciation of ob-
stetrical realities.[25] In this as in other things, Bloom assumes the
Toby role, and Stephen, a modified Walter stance:

> Of all the riddles of a married life, said my father, cross-
> ing the landing, in order to set his back against the wall, whilst
> he propounded it to my uncle *Toby* — of all the puzzling rid-
> dles, said he, in a marriage state,—of which you may trust me,
> brother *Toby*, there are more asses' loads than all *Job's* stock of
> asses could have carried — there is not one that has more in-
> tricacies than this — that from the very moment the mistress
> of the house is brought to bed, every female in it, from my la-
> dy's gentlewoman down to the cinder-wench, becomes an inch

> taller for it; and give themselves more airs upon that single
> inch, than all the other inches put together.
>
>   I think rather, replied my uncle *Toby*, 'tis we who sink an
> inch lower.—If I but meet a woman with child—I do it—'Tis
> a heavy tax upon that half of our fellow-creatures, brother
> *Shandy*, said my uncle *Toby*—'Tis a piteous burden upon 'em,
> continued he, shaking his head. — Yes, yes, 'tis a painful
> thing—said my father, shaking his head too—but certainly
> since shaking of heads came into fashion, never did two heads
> shake together, in concert, from two such different springs.
> God bless   'em all—said my uncle *Toby* and my
> Deuce take   father, each to himself.
>
> (TS 250–51)

    This striking contrast between the brothers, reiterated in Oxen as a contrast not only between Bloom and Stephen, but between Bloom and everyone else in the room, points up yet another facet of parallel and contrasting characterization. As the brothers apparently shake their heads in a concert of dismay, Sterne takes pains to point out that the reasons for their common expressions are diametrically opposed. One brother is moved by self-pity, the other by commiseration with the other half of the human race. The head-shaking is reminiscent of the joint urination in Ithaca, in which Joyce playfully suggests the union of two opposite characters.

    I do not mean to imply that all of Stephen's motives are purely selfish, or that all of Bloom's are selfless. The important thing here is the replication of a congruent act, in *Tristram Shandy* that of shaking heads. During the day Bloom and Stephen perform a number of similar acts, culminating in their mutual micturition. Also they consider many of the same topics. Stephen would save Ireland, for instance, by creating a new literary conscience for the race; Bloom, by apportioning interest-bearing money to each infant at birth, and by creating communal soup kitchens.

As we go through *Ulysses* noting similar activities and motifs, there is a tendency to metamorphose the characters of Bloom and Stephen, just as there is a similar penchant for lumping Walter and Toby together as eccentrics. The contrasts between the pairs, however, are perhaps more informative than their similarities. Common situations and motifs provide vehicles for just such informative contrasts, at the same time that they stress the common plight of mankind from Odysseus to Bloom, or from Oedipus to Willy Loman.

The more incongruous the ideas or situations, the more apparent the contrasts and similarities become, and the more comic pleasure and instruction we derive from them. For instance, Walter Shandy's literalness in attempting to identify the specific area of the body wherein the soul resides is analogous to Bloom's in attempting to feel the yellowness of his navel. The lesson in the humor is that of a literal mentality pursuing properties or essences in incongruous places.

Joyce, especially, played such games with motifs. When I was younger, I and a number of critics fell prey to Joyce's comic manipulations when we translated a collation of Epps's soluble cocoa into the transubstantiated wine and wafer, and the joint urination into the transmigration of souls. Joyce, however, had enough of Mulligan's comic skepticism to allow me a present paraphrase of Mother Grogan's wisdom—when they make water, they make water, and when they make cocoa, they make cocoa. Of course Joyce's intent to convey importance to the events of Ithaca was there, but it was a comic intent, which refrains from somber axioms regarding the divine scheme of things, and instead concerns itself with far more realistic truths. This, above all else, Joyce shared with his comic predecessors.

The Eye of the Beholder
Reader Response and Dante

*D*isheveled, gaunt Fritz Senn came from the jury box, bearing a camera, to speak once again of how the two opening words of *Ulysses* contradict each other. It was the best and the worst of times at the second Miami Joyce Birthday Celebration, that morning in the Law School Moot Court, and the text of Senn's sermon was the same as tonsured, Apollonian Berni Benstock's had been in Zurich ten years earlier: the supposed tension between *stately* and *plump* was again ingeniously pressed into service to support the idea of masterful linguistic tensions and purposeful ambiguity. In the mind of imposing, corpulent Zack Bowen, there has never been the least contradition, tension, or ambiguity between two terms that to normal people should follow as night after evening, the first the natural consequence of the second. When I raised my cogent objections on those two occasions, each time they produced smiles before the serious business at hand was readdressed. My remarks, delivered with a mixture of heartfelt sincerity and disingenuous levity, had forked no intellectual lightning, nor had they changed anyone's opinion in the ten intervening years.

What I hope makes the preceding paragraph slightly humorous to most readers is that after the discussion of comic theory and comic predecessors, reader response plays a paramount role in determining what is or is not comic, and whatever I have said will not finally convince those without a proper previous bias that *Ulysses* is a comic novel. On the other hand, I can think of only a handful of people who apparently think that there is nothing funny in it at all. We have been rightfully conditioned by Aristotle to gauge tragedy in terms of personal response, and the same judgmental process is doubly applicable to comedy, because the line between normal and comic activities and attitudes is so much more ambiguous. Actions that cause pity and terror are serious in the extreme, but actions that provoke mirth run from the bizarre through the incongruous to the mundane, and not all of those conditions are necessarily funny.

If, on the other hand, I thought that comedy were entirely in the eye of the beholder, there would have been little profit in writing a book such as this. Sometimes a joke must be explained to be regarded as funny, and the spontaneity of the humor lost in the explication is never recaptured. That is the risk run here. What I have attempted to recapture and perhaps even refine and put into historical context is what I think is the original response of most Joyce readers: that *Ulysses,* while it is a serious book and a major work of literary genius, is also a genuinely funny book and a fitting comic predecessor to *Finnegans Wake,* and that the propensity to parodic comedy hinted at in *Dubliners,* which turned to irony in *Portrait,* returned to its ancient roots in *Ulysses,* roots which were to grow and nourish the comic experimentation of the *Wake.*

Still, one work of a highly serious nature, though it contains humorous passages and the term *comedy* in its title, is rarely thought of as a funny poem. I refer, of course, to *The Divine Comedy.* A number of studies have traced parallel structures, characters, metaphors, and themes between Joyce's work and Dante's, and since Mary Reynolds's authoritative *Joyce and Dante* established definitive connections between the two authors, associations such as the ones I intend to advance in this chapter no longer seem as speculative.[1] My intent in seeing parallels between *The Divine Comedy* and *Ulysses* is primarily to demonstrate the comic potential of such seemingly incongruous parallels, and second, to suggest that Joyce's parody was directed toward not only language but also situations, characters, and themes in serious as well as in comic works. The more incongruous the parallel, of course, the greater its comic potential.

In the chapter on language I have assumed that most readers would agree that Joyce's parodic ingeniousness in the later episodes was an unmistakable indication of comic intent, and in the comic predecessors chapter I have tried to indicate that the character and situations of the earlier chapters, especially those dominated by Bloom, were not only comic in their own right, but followed in a comic tradition beginning in antiquity and sustaining itself in the earliest novels of the Renaissance and the eighteenth century. Certainly a case could also be made for similarities among the fiction of other major comic writers of the intervening centuries, but here, as with Sterne's novels, direct influences on Joyce are even harder to establish, because the later writers were themselves operating in full cognizance of a comic tradition. But that tradition did not end with Joyce, and although many successors have paid homage to his influence, the search for direct borrowings or allusions becomes more problematical as the canon of comedy swells with the years.

Once one is predisposed to look for comic echoes in later works, the imperative of reader response again takes over, and *Ulysses* is everywhere. I am not naïve enough to claim any direct borrowings or patterns either by or from Joyce, especially when they are undocumented by either Joyce's or his successors' direct acknowledgments, and I suspect that even when such admissions exist they are to be treated with caution. However, like an old evangelical preacher who has a biblical text for every situation he encounters, I have an obsession for seeing echoes of

Ulysses cropping up in many or most of the best modern comic writers' works. These writers also are totally aware of the comic tradition in which Joyce participated, and one on which I feel he had a pervasive influence. For instance, E. M. Forster's reincarnation-metempsychosis conclusion to *A Passage to India* shares with *Ulysses* its dependency on ancient comic ritual, as do several of John Barth's comic works, some of which admittedly have Joycean influences.

Joyce's experimentation caused a reconsideration of what, if any, universally accepted meaning was possible from a given set of linguistic signals. *Ulysses* and the *Wake* paved the way for the linguistic experimentation associated with meaning in the works of the best contemporary comic writers, such as Aldous Huxley, Joseph Heller, Thomas Pynchon, and Vladimir Nabokov, while Joyce's frustrated artists find their successors in such character types in the works of Joyce Cary, Kingsley Amis, and Flannery O'Connor. Nabokov, Pynchon, and Barth also share with Joyce an affinity for the most mundane aspects of contemporary pop culture juxtaposed against classical themes and intelligence, but I can't think of a comparable successor to Bloom in any contemporary comic novel, perhaps because I don't want to think he can ever be eclipsed. If ingenious linguistic incongruity was the principle mechanism of Joyce's great comic masterpiece, Leopold Bloom was its heart and soul.

THE DIVINE COMEDY

Although both tragedy and comedy assume an order to life and the universe in which it is lived, the chaos opposing that order is apparently more malevolent in tragedy. The balance is generally righted in both forms, but comedy nearly always supposes the all-pervading presence of proportion against which to measure the comic extent of the deviations from the norm. In each genre the protagonists generally attempt to do their best in an often hostile world, but more frequently in tragedy protagonists have to decide between the lesser or greater good or evil of two nearly equal alternative courses of action. Should Oedipus let the truth go begging and his city die, or pursue a search which will finally prove his undoing? Should Hamlet commit a murder to avenge a murder?

The protagonists' choices are less difficult in comedy, in part because the stakes are lower, and in part because the sense of equilibrium is never far removed from either the protagonist or the audience. Imbalance in the form of incongruity is the very basis of comic action. The return to the norm in comedy is achieved perhaps not without pain, but usually without a dimension of suffering that exceeds the joy of returning to the norm. Although tragedy evokes a sense of justice, we and the protagonists greet it with a sense of inevitability rather than with joy.

Whatever Dante suffers in the dark wood of error and in his sadness over the punishments of his romantic and literary counterparts and acquaintances, it is nothing compared to his sense of joy in his eventual salvation. Throughout, Dante's elaborate sense of design, of meticulous, balanced, numerical structure, reinforces the readers' awareness of divine and inviolable purpose. Lost in the dark wood of his complexities, those same readers are often hard put to realize the nature of the design of an artist who stands at least slightly behind or beyond or above his handiwork, partially refined out of existence, though ostensibly the work records a history of his own experience. The parallel to Joyce's work is, I think, obvious. Mary Reynolds has already pointed out the similarities between *Portrait* and the *Vita Nuova*.[2] The complexities of design in *Ulysses* rival Dante's, but are complicated even more by the focus of the spiritual journey shifting between two journeyers, Bloom and Stephen, with a subsequent confusion of the roles of Dante and Virgil.

The traditional scholarly view is that Dante called his work a comedy not only because it began in misery and ended in happiness, but also because it gave him the leeway to incorporate a variety of styles from the lowest to the most lofty and sustained. Common language raised to artistic genius throughout the *Inferno* yields to the loftier and more refined expressions of the upper realms in the later books. Joyce's shift from a superb new language of realism in the early episodes to the ingenious mimicry of the later runs along a similarly diverging track. Again, Joyce's use of such a wide variety of parodic and hence comic language provides the most obvious claim one could make for his comic intent. One difference between the two writers is that the loftier Joyce's language becomes, the funnier is his novel, while Dante's seriousness seems to increase as his rhetoric elevates.

There are scenes in both works where obvious comic intent serves pragmatic purposes, such as Dante's ludicrous figure in Cantos 21 and 22 of *The Inferno,* when in the episode of the grafters he cowers before the rough jokes of the winged devils of traditional folklore. There the intentionally comic message has to do with the poet's autobiography and his suffering unfounded accusations of misappropriation of public funds. These infernal highjinks do not seem particularly funny to this modern reader. Similarly, in *Ulysses,* jokes intended by the characters themselves to provoke mirth, such as Bloom's story of Reuben J. Dodd, or Lenehan's "Rows of cast steel," though they provide a comic atmosphere to the funeral procession and the newspaper office, are far less funny to the reader than are Bloom's speculation on cemetery copulations or the incongruity of the headlines in Aeolus, partly because in both cases the professed jokes reinforce the marginal position their tellers occupy in the company. Bloom and Lenehan try fruitlessly to gain status with their company by comic recitations which ultimately fail to redeem the tellers in their companions' eyes.

The point is that the terms *comic* and *funny* are not completely interchangeable, and that the difference generally lies in the reaction of the audience. When Dante posits a beatific journey through the underworld, the mount of earthly paradise, and the ethereal, the serious purpose hardly raises the reader's expectations of deriving much hilarity from the trip. But in the hands of another sort of comic writer, one whose intent is to produce mirth, a similar parodic journey can be extraordinarily funny, especially if the reader realizes the highly serious, even occasionally ludicrous, pretensions of the model on which it is based.

Mary Reynolds's summary and exemplification of the parallels between the *Portrait* poet, Stephen, and the early Dante of the *Vita Nuova* have encapsulated and expanded four decades of critical speculation about the influences of Dante on the early Joyce's work, and will not be reiterated here. The similarities between the autobiographical aspects of their work and the characters' devotion to their inspirational women are readily apparent. The aggregate is certainly enough to lead us to see Stephen as a Dante figure in an earthly comedy of Dublin. Any experienced reader of Joyce will be wary of pushing parallels into congruences, however, for the one verifiable aspect of Joyce's grand symmetrical design is its lack of total consistency with any earlier model. If the Dante figure of *Ulysses* is Stephen at the beginning, it is Bloom by the end. If Bloom is initially Stephen's Virgil in the beginning, the novel becomes Bloom's comic spiritual biography somewhere in the final episodes. Protean transformations make sloppy identifications and even sloppier parallels, but essential correspondences abound.

Daytime Dublin is in a supra-metaphoric sense the dark wood of Stephen's wandering, replete with such unredeemed false prophets as the Orangeman, Deasy, whose solution to Stephen's plight is frugality and to Ireland's problems, another *Resurrection of Hungary* proposal for foot-and-mouth disease in Ireland's cattle. The city is a mass of contradictions, false witnesses, blasphemous and false priests, greed, incontinence, violence, and lust, from the first scene involving Mulligan's ecclesiastical parody to his ribald solutions for Irish infertility. Yet the Dublin we see strikes most of us as not being so bad. We certainly go there on enough pilgrimages, as if it were a Joycean holy city. And even today we are amused at contemporary echoes of the very sins that Joyce has so realistically portrayed for us in his novel. If they were so bad then, why are the same traits so lovable to us now? Probably because they are a part of Joyce's universal comic drama, which is capable of seeing Dante's island with its earthly paradise summit as Ireland, crowned by the innocent garden of Howth Hill, and the bower upstairs in Number 7 Eccles Street, an upside-down view of bliss, ornamented with flakes of Plumtree's Potted Meat and inhabited by an inspirational figure whose transformational power can turn Howth into Gibraltar, Bloom into Mulvey, and a red rose into a white. But more of this presently.

Both Dante and Stephen are led through a contemporary version of history and the literature of the past to new artistic stases. Stephen's may only result in a Pisgah Sight of Palestine, a view hardly commensurate with Dante's great vision, but one which by comic extension allowed Joyce to write *Ulysses*. Both Dante's poem and Joyce's novel are in a sense reflexive, consisting of the instructive adventures of characters who are acknowledged to be poets. The fictive result of Dante's journey, delivered in retrospect by the poet-narrator, is *The Divine Comedy* itself. Certainly there are enough hints of a parallel situation in Joyce's novel to make a substantial number of critics believe that Joyce was at least playfully creating the impression that *Ulysses* was written by the Joyce-surrogate character, Stephen.

Three characters exchange roles as Dante's guides: Virgil, Beatrice, and St. Bernard, while in *Ulysses* Bloom and Stephen exchange roles as guide and tourist, with Molly serving as general goddess in charge of inspiration, assisted, like Beatrice, by three women: Mrs. Breen, who, like the Blessed Virgin, provides compassion; Gerty MacDowell, whose realm, like Rachel's, is the contemplative life; and Martha Clifford, who provides Saint Lucia's divine light and inspiration ("Young woman ... To aid gentleman in literary work" [*U* 8:524, 531–32; 1961:165]).

As William York Tindall first pointed out, both Stephen and Bloom variously fit the role of Dante.[3] If Molly has plans to provide Stephen with fleshy inspiration, but never gets a chance, she does afford a great deal of romantic inspiration for Bloom, whose masturbation, though initiated by the sight of Gerty MacDowell's drawers, culminates in thoughts of his wife's adultery. Martha, Bloom's putative literary muse, is herself inspirationally titillated by her prospective rivalry with Molly. Lizzie Twigg gives up her chance to join the company of immortal inspirers of Bloom's literary endeavors (his experiences, let us say, in a cabman's shelter), because her own literary efforts "had the good fortune to meet with the approval of the eminent poet A. E. (Mr. Geo. Russell)" (*U* 8:331–32; 1961:160). Twigg's efforts in fact were historically immortalized in a series of published poems in *The United Irishman* and in the 1905 volume *Songs and Poems,* published under an Irish nom de plume, *Elis ni Chraoibhin.*

If Stephen and Bloom move around through an unredeemed world during the day, it is also a world of pagan culture, not unlike Dante's Limbo. Bloom has recourse to improving his mind in the corresponding twin citadels of human reason and artistic endeavor in Dublin, the museum and the library, where he cogitates on the similarity of divine and human form, and Stephen discourses with the great minds of the unredeemed on the topic of Shakespeare. Though Bloom has caught a glimpse of Stephen earlier from the funeral carriage, their first contact occurs in the library. Bloom has, in a bit of dramatic foreshadowing, already led a Stephen surrogate, the blind piano tuner, across the street past the library, but he returns to the library, himself in search of a worldly rather than a spiritual direction, a model for the Keyes advertisement, with all its obvious symbolism of the lost crossed keys of the two seeker-learners. Stephen, in the role of Virgil, engages with the other unredeemed in a long, often spurious, conversation about the interaction between writers and their work, a dialogue which involves the interchangeability of fathers and sons, and artists' lives and their art. In the *Divine Comedy* Virgil assumes a patriarchal father's role in offering instruction, protection, and experience to his still-living artistic progeny, presumably as on one level Bloom offers the same to Stephen. But Bloom also is alive and certainly as influenced by Stephen's company as Stephen is his. While Bloom is no more privy to Stephen's discourse with the literary luminaries than Dante is to whatever Virgil has to tell Aristotle and company, still the subjects of literary antiquity, *Hamlet* and Shakespeare, do bear on Bloom's own search for a son-surrogate.

The next meeting between Bloom and Stephen, in the Holles Street Hospital, occurs in conjunction with the gestation and eventual contemporary dissolution-rebirth of literary language, culminating in a tawdry comic metaphor of salvation in a cough mixture. The realistic language of Dowie's message, rising from the ashes of the earlier literary parodies and succeeded by contemporary gobbledygook, is exactly the spectrum of linguistic material with which contemporary comic authors like Joyce work. Its incongruity forms the comic medium and shapes the vision the modern artist parodies. In such a comic guise, even Bloom's triteness and clichés, mimicked in Eumaeus, become comic masterpieces.

Circe is, of course, the Inferno proper. Here sin, punishment, and anguish are the reenactments of the psyche, their grotesque forms rising from the nature of the infractions, real and imagined. That the exaggerated images of the libido in Circe are also the distortions of comic incongruity trivializes and belies their basically sinful nature. Stephen's anguish about his mother is real, his punishment by the military unwarranted, but our sense of proper retribution for his and more particularly for Bloom's sinful and salacious acts, thoughts, and inclinations is far more pleasant and funny than serious. Like the *Inferno*, Circe provides comedy, but unlike the Dante cantos, Joyce's comedy is sustained throughout the chapter. For example, Mary Reynolds's detailed description of Virag as an ominous creature out of the *Inferno* fails to take into consideration that the frightening aspects of Dante's bestial figure are completely mitigated in Circe by the comic aspect of an unredeemed libidinous old man, a stock comic character long before Chaucer.[4] And we gain some comfort at the end of Circe, when Bloom reassumes the Virgilian role, covering Stephen's breakage fees, bailing him out with Kelleher and the constabulary, and taking the swooned poet into his protective custody.

The sojourners are, however, not through all of the *Inferno* yet. The lowest region is reserved for the fraudulent, the liars and ultimately the betrayers of the Eumaeus chapter. The language of the episode is principally circumlocution, the tales false, the characters frauds in one way or another, from the fraudulent traveler, D. B. Murphy, to the murderous conspirator, Skin-the-Goat Fitzharris. The concluding mute eloquence of the horse's three culminating turds again underscores the essentially comic nature of fraud. What was in Dante's eyes the most heinous of sins becomes to the comic author merely horse manure. The travelers, still discussing widely disparate music, are blended together by the narrator in one saucy little tune about a jaunting car, a song with a gross double entendre in its chorus, which purports to be about marriage, but which has little to do with anything except the driver's looking after Stephen and Bloom. They are not off to be married, even metaphorically, and they are not riding in a car. The song serves as merely the last in a long list of irrelevancies, semi-truths, and frauds in general.

Ithaca is the novel's *Purgatorio,* with its great catechistic lessons of the mountain, its sanctifying cocoa, its grand procession from the kitchen to the Edenic back yard, its detailed contemplation of the heavens, and its bower of bliss, transformed by Plumtree's Potted Meat. The learning ritual of question and answer has, as we have seen in an earlier chapter, produced little real light, but much comedy. The procession to the yard was a late Dantean addition to the episode, as Reynolds has noted. Her comments on the processional motif also place the action in a comic vein:

> The little processional takes its substance and its form from Bloom's Jewishness and Stephen's fixation on Catholic rites. It is a comic moment in the narrative, because Bloom and Stephen are going outdoors to urinate. But they are also going outdoors to say goodbye to each other. (The compositional mode of the farewell scene recalls ... the leave-taking of Dante and Virgil.) Stephen's thoughts, possibly including a recollection that Dante used the line from Psalm 113, are extended by his author into a succinct picture that enlarges the existential moment by an implicit textual union linking the old and the new dispensation. Dante's syncretism becomes an aspect of Joyce's novel.[5]

Once the egress from the house to the penumbra of the garden is effected by the travelers, they are able to contemplate unobstructed the celestial bodies and the visible luminous sign of Molly's own trip to the chamber pot, projected, like the images in Plato's cave, on the window shade by the light of a paraffin lamp. As their rivers of urine wash over the garden, the revelation in the window is accompanied by a shooting star in the heavens. Molly clearly assumes the role of inspirational figure here, and if Stephen's last look at the light through the blind darkly will not completely qualify him for the ultimate Dantean vision of God, Bloom at least will have the benefit of Molly's celestial company among the jingling quoits of the bower. It is difficult to construe the scene, especially in the light of Dante's vision, in anything other than comic terms.

The train stops at Eden, and the rest of the journey to Paradiso is a projection of Molly's Beatrice-like inspiration. Reynolds rejects Molly as a Beatrice figure because Molly chooses the red or earthly rose over the white. While Reynolds rightly points out that Molly's question "Shall I wear a white rose?" was added by Joyce late in the composition of the book, and apparently echoed Dante's "pure rose" of the opening of Canto 31 of the *Paradiso*, she fails to add that the question about the rose was also the title of a popular song of the day, a tune that Molly remembers singing in anticipation of her first appointment with Mulvey.[6] Joyce was not above letting the implications of both interpretations reverberate through the soliloquy, any more than he would have wanted any one idea to exclude another. Our comic Beatrice was indeed the earthly Joycean antidote for the sterility of heavenly virginity which looks to essences rather than flesh for its ultimate realities. The point is that Molly as pure virginal inspiration would have been as dry as the heavenly Beatrice. Rather, Molly spells out in graphic detail her proposed method of inspiring the young poet and the glorious verse which would subsequently immortalize her. Joyce's love for Dante was not above transforming Dante's medieval piety into contemporary comedy. Much of the transformation must ultimately come from the mind of a cooperative modern reader, whose view of the parallels should include a metamorphosis of serious salvation into a parody with comic intent.

Molly's soliloquy appears to revert to an earlier, if punctuated, form of narration in the novel, a return to opaque but not impenetrable verbiage. Failing elsewhere to derive any deathless message from the events of June sixteenth, we appeal to a final detached voice for the clarifying overview. Molly has been granted a special status in the book from nearly all the characters who think or speak of her, from the crowd in Flynn's to Poldy's constant appeals to her judgment. Even if the reader does not regard her as an inspirational or earth figure, her influence looms over most of her husband's activities. Her final overview of events, while characterized by the clichés of a mundane mind largely self-consumed and in constant search of her own gratification, has been variously translated into a spectrum of truths about breakfast and the cosmos which reflect not so much on the novel as on the readers' mind-sets. Her spirit may have provided an inspirational link to the first of a new generation of comic successors.

Whether or not we are able to read any sort of ultimate meaning from *Ulysses,* we still must consider whether Joyce's shift to parodic comic narration signals a shift in his values or aims. The seeming abandonment of a predominant narrative line for a variety of parodic structures did not presage a Rabelaisian abandonment of structure, or any carelessness or inconsistencies within the novel. What we have learned about Joyce's meticulous composition of the work—his painstaking revisions and constant reworking of the early episodes to conform to the later—only reinforces our belief in his precise planning and the continuity of his novel. Clearly the book shifts from Stephen's youthful, serious, romantic perspective to Bloom's middle-aged responsibilities and cares, a less dramatic attitude which in its commonplace hopes and fears seems potentially less calamitous and more comic. All this is narrated in a language increasingly idiosyncratic and imitative to the point of comic incongruity, a view of life from a series of omniscient authorities themselves perverted by comic imitation, a ready-made succession of narrators whose eccentricities call attention to themselves while they profess to relate the realistic activities of the plot. Thus while the plot remains straightforward and even a little dull, the method of relating it assumes the burden of innovation, parody, and hence comic incongruity, all the time promising some answers, some meaning, but by its very nature inhibiting any presumed meaning from surfacing. The technique just described has to be reflexive, ultimately playful, and hence comic.

This brings us back to the related issue of whether comedy can have a serious intent: whether the use of comedy as a corrective for excessive seriousness is in itself a solemn undertaking. Can and should we ultimately attempt to bring about a neutral Apollonian response toward life, neither comic nor tragic? Northrop Frye describes a continuum of seasons in the comic spring, the romantic summer, the tragic autumn, and the ironic or satiric winter, with each season so closely associated with its surrounding seasons as to be often indistinguishable, but contrasting with its opposite.[7]

Frye's approach does not take seriousness as the special province of any season, but does allow for the opposites of comedy and tragedy to correct each other's imbalance in romantic optimism on one hand and satiric or ironic didacticism on the other. Through this study I have regarded the satiric as a comic corrective and the ironic as a tragic corrective, but of course the line is never so clear. The demarcations are further blurred by the technique of parody, which I have claimed for the province of comedy, though it stands midway between comedy and satire on Frye's eternal seasonal wheel. I have claimed parody as a comic device because my point has been to differentiate between what is funny and what is grim, and I think I am typical in seeing parody as principally mirth-provoking.

When Sophocles put Oedipus into a political and personal position in which the protagonist simply couldn't walk away and let his city die or his self-image deteriorate, the playwright seemed to confirm the preordination of suffering and sorrow, and Aristotle seemed to imply that there must be some reason for the pain, some flaw like original sin, which validates such human distress. Because Oedipus was more noble than the audience in Aristotelian terms, he stuck it out through the final revelations and their concomitant pain. But most people by Aristotle's definition are not as good as Oedipus, and most of us would have gotten away, avoided the issues, taken the family, and retired to Corfu. Only in the extreme circumstances of tragedy do Oedipus's actions seem remotely justified, and those circumstances are not any more the daily fare of common man than are endless bacchanalian pleasures. The higher human values associated with tragedy always bring pain, and since there exists in humans the desire to aspire to such values, they are proportionately attracted to that pain. Hence scholars, traditionally identifying great works of literature with those values, satisfy their needs by reading them into all literature they consider great. The importance of the trivial and the common, acknowledged in English literature at least since Chaucer, has become a rallying point of modernism, but scholars still look for the uplifting eternal verities, even though they might have a difficult time pinning them down in *Ulysses* and have mercifully given them up for the most part in *Finnegans Wake*. In their search to redeem *Ulysses* through interpretations of high sentence and seriousness, the common becomes the profound, the humor assumes serious import, and the conviction that something meaningful (that is, serious) must have happened permeates the criticism. If profound meaning is difficult to find, then its very lack must reflect the sort of existential negativism that Jung first read into the book in the early thirties.[8] Reader response is everything.

Whether Dante's *Comedy* is comic any more than Panurge's grotesque and humiliating jokes are funny today is all in the mind of the reader. Certainly neither Dante nor Rabelais provokes much laughter among the sophomores in my survey of world literature class. There is incongruity and shock perhaps, but most recognize that the intent of comedy is far broader than merely provoking mirth. However, it need not necessarily aspire to those higher notions with which so many critics have endowed

Ulysses. The problem of dealing with authorial intention is in identifying the critic's intent in his or her interpretation of the author's intent. Did Joyce intend *Ulysses* to be funny? Did Rabelais, Cervantes, or Sterne have the same intentions for their works? We can speak with more surety about Sterne in this regard than any of the others, and perhaps with least assurance about Joyce.

Joyce's protagonist is a genuinely undistinguished man. Perhaps that is why he is unique among comic characters. Parson Adams, Tom Jones, The Wife of Bath, Uncle Toby were really extraordinary characters with idiosyncrasies that set them as much apart from common men as Oedipus was from his audience. Even Shakespeare's comic characters were uniquely boisterous or phlegmatic, or characterized by some disproportionate attitude or sensibility. We are hard-pressed to make any such claims for Bloom. Yet, as Hugh Kenner has often said, we know Bloom better than any other character in English literature. His very lack of heroism in the traditional sense urges us to regard his common decency, his anger at the Citizen and the rest, as a brand of heroism with which we all can identify, and his acts during Bloomsday as those which we ourselves might perform. If he were defeated by the circumstances of not being accepted by his fellow citizens, by his failure to sell any ads, by the rejection of his proffered surrogate-fatherhood to Stephen, or by his wife's infidelity, then the novel would certainly not be a comedy. There are very few readers who ever held that Bloom went to bed a beaten man, any more than a triumphal one. The book's realism denies any such conclusions. He does survive, and with a certain dignity and integrity. If he, in full knowledge of his own failings and the forces against him, is not devastated by the day's events, there is no reason for us to read it otherwise.

Notes

PREFACE

1. Carl Gustav Jung, "*Ulysses:* A Monologue," first published in the *Europaische Revue* (Berlin) 8, no. 2/9 (September 1932):547–66. The present translation is by W. Stanley Dell, as reprinted in *The Spirit of Man, Art, and Literature,* vol. 15 of Bollingen Series 20: *The Collected Works of Jung,* ed. Herbert Head, Michael Fordham, and Gerhard Adler (New York: Pantheon, 1966), 114.

2. Ibid., 114.

3. Stuart Gilbert, *James Joyce's "Ulysses,"* (New York: Vintage, 1955), ix.

4. Darcy O'Brien, "Some Psychological Determinants of Joyce's View of Love and Sex," in Fritz Senn, ed., *New Light on Joyce from the Dublin Symposium* (Bloomington: Indiana University Press, 1972), 23–24.

5. Robert Adams, *James Joyce: Common Sense and Beyond* (New York: Random House, 1966), 171, 215.

6. Cheryl Herr, "Art and Life, Nature and Culture, *Ulysses,*" in *Joyce's Ulysses: The Larger Perspective* (Newark: Univ. of Delaware Press, 1987), 19–20.

7. William York Tindall, *James Joyce: His Way of Interpreting the Modern World* (New York: Grove Press, 1950), 125–26.

A BIOLOGICAL AND CULTURAL APPROACH

1. Richard Ellmann, *Ulysses on the Liffey* (New York: Oxford University Press, 1972), xi.

2. Suzanne K. Langer, "The Comic Rhythm," in *Feeling and Form* (New York: Scribner's, 1953), 326–50.

3. Francis Macdonald Cornford, *The Origin of Attic Comedy*, ed. Theodore H. Gaster (Garden City, N.Y.: Doubleday, 1961), 9–15.

4. Langer, 348.

5. Ibid., 350.

ULYSSES AND COMIC THEORY

1. Mikhail Bakhtin, *Rabelais and His World*, Helene Iswolsky, trans. (Cambridge, Mass.: MIT Press, 1968), 4.

2. Ibid., 10.

3. Ibid., 28.

4. Ibid., 34.

5. Mark Shechner, *Joyce in Nighttown: A Psychoanalytic Inquiry into "Ulysses"* (Berkeley and Los Angeles: University of California Press, 1974).

6. Cornford, 180.

7. Bakhtin, *Rabelais*, 10.

8. Northrop Frye, *Anatomy of Criticism* (Princeton: Princeton University Press, 1971), 169–70.

9. Ibid., 171. See also Elliot Gose's excellent discussion of Saturnalia, *The Transformation Process in Joyce's "Ulysses"* (Toronto: University of Toronto Press, 1980), 147–48. Gose sees Bloom in Circe bringing his role of Lord of Misrule to a climax with his promises of Saturnalia activities such as "weekly carnivals with masked licence . . . free love," etc. (*U* 15:1690, 1693). For Bloom's role as scapegoat-clown-king, see Gose, 148, and David Hayman, "Forms of Folly in Joyce: A Study of Clowning in *Ulysses*," *ELH* 34 (1967):260–83.

10. Frye, 169.

11. Ibid., 180.

12. Ibid., 166.

13. Robert Alter, *Partial Magic: The Novel as a Self-Conscious Genre* (Berkeley and Los Angeles: University of California Press, 1975), 23.

14. Frye, 168.

15. Ibid., 179.

16. Ibid., 164.

17. Lane Cooper, *An Aristotelian Theory of Comedy with an Adaptation of "The Poetics" and a Translation of the "Tractatus Coislinianus"* (New York: Harcourt, Brace & Co., 1922); James Kern Feibleman, *In Praise of Comedy: A Study in Its Theory and Practice* (New York: Russell & Russell: 1939); and Richard Janko, *Aristotle on Comedy: Towards a Reconstruction of Poetics II* (Berkeley and Los Angeles: University of California Press, 1984).

18. Janko, 93.

19. Hugh Kenner, "Molly's Masterstroke," *James Joyce Quarterly* 10 (Fall 1972):19–28.

20. Henri Bergson, "Laughter," in Wylie Sypher, ed., *Comedy* (1956; reprint, Baltimore: Johns Hopkins University Press, 1984), 59–190.

21. Feibleman, 53.

22. Ibid., 25; Wylie Sypher, "The Meanings of Comedy," in *Comedy* (1956; reprint, Baltimore: Johns Hopkins University Press, 1984), 191–255.

23. Elder Olson, *The Theory of Comedy* (Bloomington: Indiana University Press, 1968), 36.

24. Cooper, 42.

25. Feibleman, 29.

26. Ibid., 181.

27. Hermione de Almeida, *Byron and Joyce Through Homer: "Don Juan" and "Ulysses"* (New York: Columbia University Press, 1981), 64–65.

28. Sypher, 201.

29. George Meredith, "An Essay on Comedy." In *Comedy*, Wylie Sypher, ed. (1956: reprint, Baltimore: Johns Hopkins University Press, 1984), 1–57.

30. Frye, 177.

31. In *Partial Magic* Alter devotes entire chapters to *Don Quixote, Tristram Shandy, Jacques,* and *Pale Fire*, relegating *Ulysses* to a chapter on a number of modern novels that revived the tradition.

32. Bergson, 170–71.

33. Sypher, 217–18.

34. Cooper, 20.

35. Sypher, 208.

36. Cooper, 75.

37. Ibid., 194.

38. Ibid., 181.

39. Feibleman, 182.

40. Cooper, 60–62.

COMIC NARRATION

1. Marilyn French, *The Book as World: James Joyce's "Ulysses"* (Cambridge, Mass.: Harvard University Press, 1976); Karen Lawrence, *The Odyssey of Style in "Ulysses"* (Princeton: Princeton University Press, 1981).

2. Robert Adams, *Surface and Symbol: The Consistency of James Joyce's "Ulysses"* (New York: Random House, 1966); Michael Groden, *"Ulysses" in Progress* (Princeton: Princeton University Press, 1977).

3. Mikhail Bakhtin, *Problems of Dostoevsky's Poetics,* Caryl Emerson, ed. and trans. (Minneapolis: University of Minnesota Press, 1984), 127.

4. Geoffrey Hartman, Letter, *PMLA* 92 (March 1977):307–8.

5. French, 140.

6. Lawrence, 106 n. 10.

7. Ibid., 144.

8. Quoted in Virginia Woolf's *A Writer's Diary: Being Extracts from the Diary of Virginia Woolf*, ed. Leonard Woolf (New York: Harcourt, Brace & Co., 1953), 39.

9. Lawrence, 170; French, 208–9.

10. Lawrence, 197–98.

11. For a detailed analysis of the role of pantomimes in Joyce see Cheryl Herr, *Joyce's Anatomy of Culture* (Urbana: University of Illinois Press, 1986), 96–135.

12. Ruth Bauerle recently made this important and as yet unpublished discovery.

COMIC PREDECESSORS

1. Hermoine de Almeida, *Byron and Joyce Through Homer: "Don Juan" and "Ulysses"* (New York: Columbia University Press, 1981).

2. Joanne E. Rea, "Rabelais and Joyce: A Study in Verbal Humor," Ph.D. Diss., University of Kentucky, 1979 (Ann Arbor: University Microfilms International, 1979); John Edward Kidd, "Joyce's Debt to Rabelais," Ph.D. Diss., University of California, Santa Cruz, 1985 (Ann Arbor: University Microfilms International, 1985). Kidd's study, which is highly speculative regarding specific textual parallels, is unconvincing in its claim that Rabelais is Joyce's "literary Siamese twin," but offers a comprehensive assessment of previous critical comparisons between the two writers and a convincing case for Joyce's having owned and read Rabelais both in the original and in the Urquhart and Motteux translation long before earlier critics had thought.

3. Joyce wrote in a May 31, 1927, letter to Harriet Shaw Weaver, "But then I never read Rabelais either though nobody will believe this. I will read them both [Lewis Carroll and Rabelais] when I get back. I read a few chapters of a book called *La langue de Rabelais*" (*Letters of James Joyce*, vol. 1, ed. Stuart Gilbert [New York: Viking, 1957], 255).

4. In Molly's soliloquy she demonstrates knowledge not only of the scene of Gargantua's birth but also of Rabelais's biography: "Like some of those books he brings me the works of Master Francois Somebody supposed to be a priest about a child born out of her ear because her bumgut fell out a nice word for any priest to write and her a— —e as if any fool wouldnt know what that meant" (*U* 18:488–91). For a more detailed discussion see Joanne E. Rea, "Joyce and 'Master François Somebody,' " *James Joyce Quarterly* 18, no. 4 (Summer 1981):445–50.

5. *Letters of James Joyce*, vol. 3, ed. Richard Ellmann (New York: Viking, 1966), 40, 44, 74n.

6. Albert Jay Nock and C. R. Wilson, *Francis Rabelais: The Man and His Work* (New York: Harper & Brothers, 1929), 260.

7. Bakhtin, *Rabelais*, 21.

8. Two excellent studies relate bodily poles and functions to Joyce's work. Lindsey Tucker's *Stephen and Bloom at Life's Feast: Alimentary Symbolism and the Creative Process in James Joyce's "Ulysses"* (Columbus: Ohio State University Press, 1984) details how body functions relate to ritual, fertility, and art, especially as they apply to Stephen and Bloom in *Portrait* and *Ulysses;* while Barbara DiBernard, in *Alchemy and "Finnegans Wake"* (Albany: State University of New York Press, 1980) analyzes Joyce's relation of the lower bodily functions to artistic creativity and alchemy in *Ulysses*, and, more important, *Finnegans Wake*. Both Tucker and DiBernard stress the antiquity of various transformational rites associated with natural bodily functions.

9. Feibleman, 52.

10. Joyce declared in a letter to Theodore Spicer-Simson (June 8, 1910) his preference for Swift and Goldsmith (*Letters of James Joyce*, vol. 2, ed. Stuart Gilbert [New York: Viking, 1967]), 285.

11. Richard Ellmann, *James Joyce* (New York: Oxford Univ. Press, 1982), 416.

12. All references to *Don Quixote* are from Samuel Putnam's two-volume translation (New York: Viking, 1949).

13. de Almeida, 42–43.

14. Alter, 2–3.

15. See Samuel Putnam's summary of this sort of negative criticism in *The Portable Cervantes*, trans. and ed. Samuel Putnam (New York: Viking, 1951), 21–22.

16. Bakhtin, *Rabelais*, 22.

17. Some of us have been discussing transformation as a major motif of the novel for decades; see Zack Bowen, *Musical Allusions in the Works of James Joyce: Early Poetry through "Ulysses"* (Albany: State University of New York Press, 1974), 56–58, and Ann Ridgeway, "Two Authors in Search of a Reader" *James Joyce Quarterly* 1, no. 4 (Summer 1964):48–50. More recent studies such as Elliot Gose's landmark *The Transformation Process in Joyce's "Ulysses"* and Lindsey Tucker's *Stephen and Bloom at Life's Feast* have delineated the scope of the transformation theme and developed its ramifications.

18. Bakhtin, *Rabelais*, 370.

19. Bowen, 63–64.

20. Lodwick Hartley, " 'Swiftly-Sterneward': The Question of Stern's Influence on Joyce," *Studies in the Literary Imagination* 3, no. 2 (October 1970):46.

21. Ridgeway, 42.

22. Ibid., 41.

23. All references to *Tristram Shandy* are from the Rinehart edition, ed. Samuel Holt Monk (New York: Rinehart, 1950).

24. Dorothy Van Ghent, "On *Tristram Shandy*," *The English Novel: Form and Function* (New York: Harper & Row, 1961), 87.

25. I am indebted to my colleague Lindsey Tucker for this interpretation of the Oxen activities.

THE EYE OF THE BEHOLDER

1. Mary Reynolds, *Joyce and Dante: The Shaping Imagination* (Princeton: Princeton University Press, 1981). Reynolds lists the major studies on pages 332–33, note 9.

2. Ibid., 183 and *passim*.

3. William York Tindall, "Dante and Mrs. Bloom," *Accent*, 11, no. 2 (Spring 1951):85–92.

4. Reynolds, 73–74.

5. Ibid., 124–25.

6. Ibid., 79.

7. Frye, 151–242.

8. Jung, "*Ulysses:* A Monologue."

Works Cited

Adams, Robert. *James Joyce: Common Sense and Beyond*. New York: Random House, 1966.

———. *Surface and Symbol: The Consistency of James Joyce's "Ulysses."* New York: Random House, 1966.

Alter, Robert. *Partial Magic: The Novel as a Self-Conscious Genre*. Berkeley: University of California Press, 1975.

Bakhtin, Mikhail. *Problems of Dostoevsky's Politics*. Edited and translated by Caryl Emerson. Minneapolis: University of Minnesota Press, 1984.

———. *Rabelais and His World*. Translated by Helene Iswolsky. Cambridge, Mass.: The MIT Press, 1968.

Bergson, Henri. *Laughter*. In *Comedy*, edited by Wylie Sypher, 59–190. 1956. Reprint. Baltimore: The Johns Hopkins University Press, 1984.

Bowen, Zack. *Musical Allusions in the Works of James Joyce: Early Poetry Through "Ulysses."* Albany: State University of New York Press, 1974.

Cervantes, Saavedra, Miguel de. *Don Quixote*. Translated by Samuel Putnam in two volumes. New York: Viking Press, 1949.

Cooper, Lane. *An Aristotelian Theory of Comedy with an Adaptation of "The Poetics" and a Translation of the "Tractatus Coislinianus."* New York: Harcourt, Brace and Company, 1922.

Cornford, Francis Macdonald. *The Origin of Attic Comedy*, edited by Theodore H. Gaster. Garden City, N.Y.: Anchor Books, Doubleday, 1961.

de Almeida, Hermione. *Byron and Joyce Through Homer: "Don Juan" and "Ulysses."* New York: Columbia University Press, 1981.

DiBernard, Barbara. *Alchemy and "Finnegans Wake."* Albany: State University of New York Press, 1980.

Ellmann, Richard. *James Joyce.* New York: Oxford University Press, 1982.

———. *Ulysses on the Liffey.* New York: Oxford University Press, 1972.

Feibleman, James Kern. *In Praise of Comedy: A Study in Its Theory and Practice.* New York: Russell & Russell, 1939.

French, Marilyn. *The Book as World: James Joyce's "Ulysses."* Cambridge, Mass.: Harvard University Press, 1976.

Frye, Northrop. *Anatomy of Criticism.* Princeton: Princeton University Press, 1971.

Gilbert, Stuart. *James Joyce's "Ulysses."* New York: Vintage, 1955.

Gose, Elliott. *The Transformation Process in Joyce's "Ulysses."* Toronto: University of Toronto Press, 1980.

Groden, Michael. *"Ulysses" in Progress.* Princeton: Princeton University Press, 1977.

Hartley, Lodwick. " 'Swiftly-Sterneward': The Question of Sterne's Influence on Joyce." *Studies in the Literary Imagination* 3 (1970): 37–41.

Hartman, Geoffrey. Letter. *PMLA* 92 (1977):307–8.

Hayman, David. "Forms of Folly in Joyce: A Study of Clowning in *Ulysses.*" *ELH* 34 (1967):260–83.

Herr, Cheryl. "Art and Life, Nature and Culture, *Ulysses.*" In *Joyce's Ulysses: The Larger Perspective,* edited by Robert D. Newman and Weldon Thornton, 19–38. Newark: University of Delaware Press, 1987.

———. *Joyce's Anatomy of Culture.* Urbana: University of Illinois Press, 1986.

Janko, Richard. *Aristotle on Comedy: Towards a Reconstruction of Poetics II.* Berkeley: University of California Press, 1984.

Joyce, James. *Letters of James Joyce,* vol. 1. Edited by Stuart Gilbert. New York: Viking, 1957.

———. *Letters of James Joyce,* vol. 2. Edited by Richard Ellmann. New York: Viking, 1966.

———. *Letters of James Joyce,* vol. 3. Edited by Richard Ellmann. New York: Viking, 1966.

Jung, Carl Gustav. "*Ulysses:* A Monologue." Translated by W. Stanley Dell. Reprinted in *The Spirit of Man Art, and Literature.* Vol. 15 of

Bollingen Series 20: *The Collected Works of Jung*, 109–34. Edited by Herbert Head, Michael Fordham, and Gerhard Adler. New York: Pantheon Books, 1966.

Kenner, Hugh. "Molly's Masterstroke." *James Joyce Quarterly* 10 (1972): 19–28.

Kidd, John Edward. "Joyce's Debt to Rabelais." Ph.D. diss., University of California, Santa Cruz, 1985.

Langer, Suzanne K. *Feeling and Form*. New York: Scribner's, 1953.

Lawrence, Karen. *The Odyssey of Style in "Ulysses."* Princeton: Princeton University Press, 1981.

Meredith, George. "An Essay on Comedy." In *Comedy*, edited by Wylie Sypher, 1–57. 1956. Reprint. Baltimore: Johns Hopkins University Press, 1984.

Nock, Albert Jay, and Wilson, C. R. *Francis Rabelais: The Man and His Work*. New York: Harper and Brothers, 1929.

O'Brien, Darcy. "Some Psychological Determinates of Joyce's View of Love and Sex." In *New Light on Joyce from the Dublin Symposium*, edited by Fritz Senn, pp. 15–27. Bloomington: Indiana University Press, 1972.

Olson, Elder. *The Theory of Comedy*. Bloomington: Indiana University Press, 1968.

Putnam, Samuel, ed. *The Portable Cervantes*. New York: Viking, 1951.

Rea, Joanne. "Rabelais and Joyce: A Study in Verbal Humor." Ph.D. diss., University of Kentucky, 1979.

Reynolds, Mary. *Joyce and Dante: The Shaping Imagination*. Princeton: Princeton University Press, 1981.

Ridgeway, Ann. "Two Authors in Search of a Reader." *James Joyce Quarterly* 1 (1964) 41–51.

Schechner, Mark. *Joyce in Nighttown: A Psychoanalytic Inquiry into "Ulysses."* Berkeley: University of California Press, 1974.

Sterne, Laurence. *Tristram Shandy*, edited by Samuel H. Monk. New York: Rinehart and Company, 1950.

Sypher, Wylie. "The Meanings of Comedy." In *Comedy*, edited by Wylie Sypher, 1956. Reprint. Pp. 191–255. Baltimore: Johns Hopkins University Press, 1984.

Tindall, William York. "Dante and Mrs. Bloom." *Accent* 11 (1951): 85–92.

———. *James Joyce: His Way of Interpreting the Modern World*. New York: Grove Press, 1950.

Tucker, Lindsey. *Stephen and Bloom at Life's Feast: Alimentary Symbolism and the Creative Process in James Joyce's "Ulysses."* Columbus: Ohio State University Press, 1984.

Van Ghent, Dorothy. *The English Novel: Form and Function.* New York: Harper & Row, 1961.

Woolf, Virginia. *A Writer's Diary: Being Extracts From the Diary of Virginia Woolf.* Edited by Leonard Woolf. New York: Harcourt, Brace & Company, 1953.

Index

ULYSSES AS A COMIC NOVEL

was composed in 10 on 13 Baskerville on a Merganthaler Linotron 202
by Partners Composition;
printed by sheet-fed offset on 50-pound, acid-free Glatfelter Natural Hi-Bulk,
Smyth-sewn and bound over binder's boards in Holliston Roxite B,
with dust jackets printed in 2 colors
by Braun-Brumfield, Inc.;
designed by Victoria Lane;
and published by

SYRACUSE UNIVERSITY PRESS

SYRACUSE, NEW YORK 13244-5160